The Journey of
the Self

The Journey of the Self

A Sufi Guide to Personality

Shaykh Fadhlalla Haeri

HarperSanFrancisco

A Division of HarperCollins*Publishers*

FIRST HARPERSANFRANCISCO PAPERBACK EDITION PUBLISHED IN 1991.

Library of Congress Cataloging-in-Publication Data

Haeri, Fadhlalla.
    The journey of the self : a Sufi guide to personality / Fadhlalla Haeri. — 1st HarperSanFrancisco pbk. ed.
        p.   cm.
    Reprint. Originally published: 1989.
    Includes bibliographical references.
    ISBN 0–06–250376–6 (alk. paper)
    1. Sufism.   I. Title
BP189.2.H34   1991
297′.4—dc20   89–46450
                                                                              CIP

---

91   92   93   94   95   HAD   10   9   8   7   6   5   4   3   2   1

This edition is printed on acid-free paper which meets the American National Standards Institute Z39.48

Contents

Acknowledgements

I am indebted to Allah's all-encompassing mercy, which has made us yearn for the path of true bliss through submission and surrender. I thank Allah for all the means and the processes of learning and experiencing along the path of love. I thank the many masters and teachers who have looked upon me kindly and affectionately. I thank Allah for the sincere friends, family and helpers who have made this book possible by their devotion, loyalty and tireless hours of editorial contribution. Those who have helped me are so many that I cannot mention them all. Batul Haeri worked continually on the manuscript with me for four years and without her, this book would not have been produced. I also wish to acknowledge Muna H. Bilgrami, Aga Abbas Bilgrami, Aga Haj Muhammad Ibrahim, Haj Mustafa, Jamila Kabira, Haj Ahmad, Rifat Nafisa, Dr Aliya and Maryam for their editorial participation, and Dr Stan Gooch and Christopher Flint for editing the text. Finally, special gratitude is expressed to Dr Robert Frager, who encouraged me in this endeavour and at whose centre the first public talk on this subject was given. I am especially grateful to him for his contribution of the foreword to this book.

Foreword

There is a great spiritual hunger today. Many people have found that their real spiritual needs and deep inner questions have not been met by conventional religious writings or institutions. Many have looked in vain to psychology to fill the functions religion used to provide. *The Journey of the Self* provides a genuine spiritual psychology that speaks directly to this spiritual hunger. It is a psychology that is rooted in an understanding of the human soul, and the relation of the soul to the rest of the psyche. It is a psychology of self-knowledge, grounded in a practical understanding of the elements of the inner spiritual journey, and grounded also in the knowledge of Reality that is behind the world as we usually know it.

This is a very special book. It introduces an old and complex psychology taken from a variety of Islamic and Sufi sources. Much of this material has never been translated before, relatively unknown even in the Middle East. *The Journey of the Self* is of real use for both practising Sufis and others interested in spiritual psychology.

Among men and women of faith, there has been serious doubt concerning the role of Western psychology for anyone with religious or mystical convictions. Traditional study of Western academic psychology often leads to a loss of faith, among both Western and Eastern students. This is the result of an unconscious acceptance of the unspoken tenets of Western psychology, which include positivism, materialism and a strong negative bias concerning religious and spiritual experience.

The antidote to this is the development of an alternative model of human nature, the development of a spiritual psychology. Any genuine spiritual psychology must proceed from a set of basic assumptions that are fundamentally different from those of traditional Western psychology. Some of these assumptions include the following:

1. Human experience includes both the sacred and the secular. Any spiritual (or full) psychology must deal with both. This also means that any spiritual psychology must deal with the relation of the individual with the Divine, with the experience of Reality that is so frequently described in the world's mystical traditions.

2. The soul or deep self is an inner mystery within each of us, and also is part of the very essence of what it is to be human. Thus, the mystical quest can be understood as an essential aspect of real human development. One of the central tasks of any spiritual psychology is to study the soul and its relation with the rest of the psyche.

3. There are various possible states of human consciousness. Waking consciousness is only one type, and other states, such as mystical states, have their own special validity. Therefore, to base a psychology on only the limited experience of 'average' people during waking is to limit drastically the range of psychology.

4. The literature of mysticism frequently describes a kind of radical self-transformation. The concept of major, qualitative change during adulthood has not been examined in Western psychology, except for negative instances, such as psychosis. From the point of view of spiritual psychology, this self-transformation is an integral part of healthy adult development, fundamental in the integration of the soul with the personality.

The Journey of the Self provides a marvellous example of spiritual psychology, and reveals an understanding of the human psyche which is rooted in faith and spiritual practice. It also provides a complex model of human nature into which we can fit various concepts and theories from academic Western psychology. This book provides the best introduction I know of to this kind of model.

I have been particularly impressed by the relationship explicated between the development of the human soul and the development of the cosmos. This dramatically demonstrates that ancient spiritual wisdom can be shown to be completely compatible with the most modern scientific theories and cosmology. In addition, a wonderful combination of spirituality and practicality have been woven throughout this volume.

It takes a rare author to write a book like this. Shaykh Fadhlalla is a man who is completely at home in the East and the West. He is a scholar and an effective and practical Sufi teacher, an international businessman and also an international philanthropist.

I had the pleasure of serving as Shaykh Fadhlalla's host several years ago, when he presented a talk to a gathering here in Redwood City, California. The talk was devoted to the model of spiritual psychology that is detailed in this book. The audience included many psychologists and therapists who were fascinated by the talk. I was deeply impressed with Shaykh Fadhlalla's humour and sensitivity, and by his familiarity with the West and all the problems of seriously pursuing a spiritual discipline in the midst of Western culture. Our people here immediately responded to him and to his talk.

We are reminded in this book again and again how much we can learn from the wisdom of the Islamic teachings and the Sufi tradition. After all, over many centuries, Sufi shaykhs have served not only as spiritual guides but also as therapists and family counsellors for their dervishes. There is much more 'clinical' wisdom and experience to be found in the Sufi and Islamic traditions than in the brief history of Western psychotherapy.

We are invited to self-understanding in this book, to psychology and spiritual self-knowledge. Not only are we invited, we are given examples and concrete help in making our way toward that goal.

Robert Frager, Ph.D
Founder, Institute for Transpersonal Psychology

Introduction

This book is an attempt to present the Western reader with a basic Islamic conception of the self. It is a concept that can be found within the revealed spiritual teachings of several world religions and, in particular, the Judaic, Christian and Islamic traditions. The knowledge and science of the self exists in the Islamic tradition in greater clarity and applicability because its teachings are more recent and have not been distorted, and they continue to be practised up to the present day.

The basis of this knowledge of the self is that all humanity is one in its essence and origin. There is a primal or basic self which is the same in all human beings. We may differ biologically but the root of our motivations in life is similar. This model of the one adamic self is the pillar of all Islamic teachings and is to be found in the Qur'an, the Prophetic traditions and the teachings of the masters and saints.

We have all come from one source, and that one essential reality pervades all dual manifestations in existence. The physical world is based on duality, and everything in nature is created in pairs of opposites. All experiences, events, causal relationships and mental and intellectual appreciation are based on experiencing those opposites. We seek to understand, balance and reconcile the experienced opposite forces, driven as we are by the awareness of the essential unity within. This inner drive is unconscious and lies beyond our intellect and reason. As full appreciation of the natural law of opposites and complementarity sets in, we move beyond intellect and reason to our original unitive state, which is innate in all of us.

Man has always been searching for a fundamental law of nature which underlies the great variety of natural phenomena. Classical physicists answered many of the physical observations through the Newtonian mechanistic model of the universe. With the development of subatomic physics as well as new advances in astrophysics, we find a disappearance of the old atomic building block. The quantum theory introduced the concept of the participation of the observer, thus making invalid the idea of an objective description of nature and the separation between the observer and the observed. It put an end to the deterministic law of nature and the absolute objectivity of scientific experimentation. In atomic physics, one cannot talk about its nature without speaking about the observer and his position.

Modern physicists are viewing the universe more and more as a unified whole which is interconnected in subtle ways. The concept of unbroken wholeness and the interdependence of mind and matter are increasingly being discussed among scientists.

It is very interesting also, to reflect upon the fact that no longer can physicists talk about space without talking about time. It is curious to think that atomic particles travelling at high speeds appear to have a longer lifespan, and that at high velocities size seems to shrink. The three-dimensional world which we experience seems like only an image or a shadow of the relativistic, four-dimensional, space-time world. Doesn't this coincide with the spiritual teachings that remind us that this world is only a shadow of reality? By focusing on the shadow and being absorbed in its motion, surely we miss the reality that is causing it. The practice of meditation and sublimation seems to produce an effect of diminishing and finally disappearance of all experiential entities. This vanishing of space brings about the disappearance of time.

The practice is that if the identifiable self – the subjective you and I – is taken away, the concept of time and space will also be sublimated. Then the original reality (of one self), which was there before, now remains without a shadow to veil it.

Nowadays contemporary physicists, as well as other scientists, are looking for an all-embracing order and unifying factor upon which physical reality is founded. More and more, cosmologists are faced with the questions of how, when and why did everything begin. There is a general consensus to answer the first two questions: 10 to 20 billion years ago the universe came into being from a non-bounded state; and, after its full expansion and the big crunch, will return once more to its original, non-bounded state. Within this cosmic overlapping a number of modes of thought and theories have been put forth, to varying degrees of accuracy, to describe it. But the ongoing pre-creational state, being non-space-time related, lies beyond the realm of contemporary science and verges on the mystical or religious type of belief or experience.

The third question, why was the universe created, also lies beyond the grasp of science. It was revealed to the Prophet Muhammad that the essence of all creation is the greatest hidden treasure, and that it loved to be known; so it created, in order that it might be known. The Islamic viewpoint is that man, being the highest of all creation, is able to qualify for that knowledge, otherwise he will remain chasing the shadow of the images within the limitation of time and space in this world, without ever achieving freedom, true contentment or satisfaction.

The path to this experiential awakening is by understanding, inner abandonment and purification. The science of the self is indispensable for the preparation of attaining inner freedom.

This life, then, is a training-ground for us to witness how perfect are the universal laws of nature which in fact drive us towards seeking that limitless source of unity. We are born with an inner tendency which constantly motivates us towards our unitive origins. Our purpose in this life is to discover and know the basic nature of the self and the spiritual foundation which underlies it. We will only attain contentment when our potential as a spiritual being is fulfilled. No matter what we do in this world, it will never be totally satisfying. In other words, no matter how hard we try to attain fulfilment, harmony and peace, in the physical, emotional or intellectual sense, we will never be satisfied.

Our conception of the self shows that life is a journey of unfolding discovery towards self-knowledge, and that knowledge begins with physical and material consciousness at birth and evolves into emotional, mental and intellectual consciousness, then culminates at maturity with higher spiritual consciousness, or pure awareness.

It is by reason of this progression that we try to obtain fulfilment, first by seeking contentment physically and materially, then emotionally, mentally and intellectually, and then spiritually; and ultimately, simply in pure contentment, which is contentment for and by itself.

Any activity that leads us towards realising our inner potential and essential nature we will find to be nourishing, enriching and conducive to fulfilment; and any other activity will be palliative, detractive to growth, and even destructive.

According to our conception of the self, then, conditions of imbalance or disturbance in the self are symptoms of something that has gone wrong in the natural progression of self-unfoldment or because of our not moving forward along the intended journey of self-discovery.

From this point of view, many who are considered in need of care could be individuals who are highly sensitive and possess greater spiritual potential than others. They may be persons who primarily need spiritual remedies and should be treated and corrected in this way, because they find the physical world does not fully answer their questions or fill their needs.

Any suffering from the world, then, could be considered as a positive experience; for it is a reminder that one is misdirecting one's energies, and could lead one back to the intended path of self-knowledge. It is for one to take corrective action – not to disconnect from one's experiential wholeness by being given chemical pills or analysis, neither of which reaches the root of the problem – which is to discover the true nature of the self.

The fact that such a large percentage of the population is currently under care, especially in highly technologised societies, is itself a positive indication that there is hope for humanity. The remedy called for is based on self-knowledge rather than the symptomatically-oriented forms of treatment which are prevalent at this time. Many people, in fact, may only be helped if they are allowed to be taught to understand this basic conception of the self and to see it manifest and working in themselves. With understanding, guidance from an awakened teacher, and a sense of humour, many may be able to overcome most of the obstacles that cause confusion or depression and an inability to cope with the world.

In Chapter One we lay down stepping-stones from which we introduce our conception of the self. Our approach touches upon a progression of life experiences, beginning at birth. Questions are posed to ask what are the basic motivations underlying all creation that make us behave as we do, and what aspects in life are by their nature common to all of us.

Chapter Two discusses the nature and spectrum of the self. We define what is meant by the self, and put forth a description of its real and basic nature.

In Chapter Three we trace the journey of the self through its five phases of development in this life towards higher consciousness, and its return to its origin. This journey is based on a pattern that charts a parallel progression of the outer (biological) and inner (conscious) development of the human being. But although the focus is on the human being (the microcosm), the phases of development are echoed in the macrocosm of the universe. These phases are meant to be seen as a general description of the flow of human development and, as such, there will necessarily be some overlapping between phases. Aspects of earlier phases remain active to varying degrees of intensity throughout one's life, even as one progresses in the journey.

Phase One is the world of Absolute Unitive Reality. It is the realm of the absolute void – timeless, eternal, infinite, unmanifest. It is the world of pure consciousness, of reality before physical creation.

Creation begins with the transition to Phase Two, Inner Dependence. Conception, pregnancy, the cosmos unfolding – this phase outlines the earliest stages of creation. In Phase Three, that of Outer Dependence, creation explodes into a discernible universe, and this is reflected in the microcosm in the birth of the human being. Here, the newborn is totally dependent outwardly.

As Phase Three moves into Phase Four, there is a gradual shift from extreme outer dependence to Interdependence with other elements. It is this phase of Interdependence which charts our growth to full physical, emotional, intellectual and cognitive maturity, and there is the greatest level of outer activity and interrelationships. It is here that we introduce grids and models that will help us to understand the basic patterns and relationships in the macrocosm of creation and in the microcosm of human behaviour.

In the transition from Phase Four to Phase Five (Inner Reliance), maturation as a rational being draws one away from the appetites and distractions of physical existence to an awakening of the inner life. In Phase Five, there is an increased awakening and reliance on inner experiences, and we can attain the highest possible station of fulfilment. While we still live, we will always be to some degree interdependent upon other beings in this world. Movement towards the spiritual life does not imply renunciation of this world, nor is the physical world a mere illusion. Its very transience impels us to see beyond it. Our experience of the next consciousness (after death) is determined by our actions and experiences in this life. In reality, the Fire of Hell and the Garden of Paradise are states of consciousness, so both can be experienced in this life before physical death. Finally, the journey in this life is completed with the return of the self to its origin.

The outline of the journey of the self in five phases has been synthesised by the author for illustration and analysis, whilst within the phases themselves teachings by other writers and masters have been included and quoted.

In Chapter Four we examine the major symptoms and conditions of the self as well as their root causes, and discuss the nature of their treatment and cure. Here we shall also examine the virtues of the self.

Finally, in Chapter Five, we illustrate the inherent unified nature of the self by examining situations that show how the self throughout its life manifests characteristics and tendencies towards its unific origin. The examples illustrate how the self is connected at all times to the unific factor that underlies it. By the variety of examples given, the reader will be able to see from personal experiences and observations the predominance of the unified nature of the self. No doubt the reader can add to our small sampling many more cases and observations.

Within this model of the self, aspects of ancient Eastern spiritual teachings as well as Middle Eastern religions or Western philosophies can be found to exist. Islam, being the primal adamic code, predates all of these teachings, although it was unveiled in its totality only fourteen centuries ago. Orientalists, for example, have referred to aspects of the Islamic teachings on the self as neoplatonic. The truth is that Plato's writings are an aspect of the adamic teachings and in themselves are incomplete.

One of the reasons that the Islamic cosmology of the self and higher consciousness is not more widely known in the West could lie in its multidimensional nature, and the difficulty of unravelling one strand from its total wholeness. The Qur'an, for example, talks about man's outer code of social responsibility and his path of inner purification in the same breath. It speaks about higher consciousness and Islamic law in parallel. It talks about this world and the next in complete harmony and relatedness. For a reader who has not accepted revealed laws in this world, it will be a greater challenge to accept or understand the Qur'an as it relates to the self and higher awareness.

The reader needs to approach this work with an open heart and without prejudice in order to benefit. These teachings can only be useful if accepted and applied; they are of little benefit for purposes of discussion, debate or similar academic pursuits.

Our conception of the self is intended for use by the layman and expert alike, as a basic foundation or blueprint for any system of self-knowledge or the psychological sciences. Irrespective of whether or not one believes in or accepts the unific reality that underpins the self and all of creation, one will still find that this conception can be applied to any system as a blueprint that explains human behaviour and provides for it remedies and cures.

The sole intention of our present work is to provide a basic model of the self, which others may then wish to take and develop further by building upon it. Usable and successful techniques that have been developed in the West over the past may be added and integrated. A review of contemporary theories and techniques can be made, and those parts which fit within this conception will be useful and will last, and those which do not fit within this conception will eventually be found not to stand the test of time and will be discarded. Others may wish to apply their knowledge and field experience to this blueprint of self-knowledge in order to develop it further towards greater applicability. This book is only a first step towards developing and evolving a comprehensive and pragmatic model of the self in this field.

Although we attempt in this work to describe all aspects of the self and its journey towards enlightenment, the achievement of this is rarely possible without a realised teacher. The enlightened person will guide others in a wise and inspired way towards the ultimate goal, whereas a treatise such as this is a mere description of the basic field of activity. In fact, a deep criticism of this work is that by our merely presenting it, it may lead the individual seeker to assume that the cure is in sight; however, having a simple, analytical knowledge of a situation is very different from actually arriving at the results.

So once the appropriate recipe for life is found, the next step is to be amongst the experts who have applied it and, thereby, have been transformed by it. There is a vast difference between reading a menu and deriving nourishment from a meal; but the sincere seeker of wisdom will end up by being amongst the wise.

1

Stepping-stones to Self-knowledge

We must build a bridge if we are to reach the intended shore. In this first chapter, we will outline the assumptions and pose questions that will orient the reader to the knowledges of the self. Each stepping-stone on the way shares with the reader an aspect of the human situation as we observe it; that is, of the basic realities and facts of the life in which we find ourselves, of the personal, social and moral factors which influence us, and of the prime motives, basic needs and impulses of the self that drive us hither and thither.

The many stepping-stones of the human situation described in the following pages form a pathway which will give us access to an understanding of the self.

The Vortex of Creation

Humanity is caught in the dynamics of life. We are driven either to satisfy our desires and impulses – be they rational or irrational – or to avoid unpleasant disturbances and conflicts. At times, we are successful in this challenge, and at other times we fail.

It can be observed that we share a great many experiences in common, as well as many differences. We will look at how this situation arises. We will also consider the meaning of the one self, the drive for knowledge, and the quest for freedom when we know we are bound, and we will examine these points and many others so that we may attain a clear understanding of the dynamics of the self and its basic essence. For until the basic fundamental nature of all humanity is fully understood, there cannot be a proper understanding of individual or collective behaviour.

The One Self

There is a primal or basic self – which can be described as patterns of expectations, desires, fears, needs and values – which is the same in all human beings. We may be different biologically and in our outer behaviour, but the root of our motivations in life is the same. This model of the one adamic self is the pillar of all Islamic teachings and is to be found in the Qur'an, the Prophetic traditions and the teachings of the masters and saints.

The Qur'an says that you were created from one self. Each individual self has a higher nature and a lower nature. We function on a spectrum which at one end resembles the lowest of animalistic impulses and thoughtless responses, and at the other end, a sublime, patient, considerate and independent yet loving and compassionate nature. We can at times behave worse than the lowest of animals, and at other times with a selflessness and nobility that cannot be surpassed. Whether we reflect our higher self or our lower self, there remains within us an unchanging, steady state of the one self, which is the same foundation in each person. When we are least subject to the changeable impulses of the self, we gain greater access to that constant one self within.

The Many Profiles but One Face of Humanity

A great diversity in character traits can be observed within the one individual – childishness, innocence, aggression, domesticity, materialism, spirituality, adventurousness, reflectiveness, impulsiveness, and so on. All of these traits and many others are harboured within one bosom. Each individual being is like a new stream produced by fresh rain. Many such streams pour forth into the ocean of humanity from which they originated. Although individuals have their own unique characteristics, biologically and environmentally related, ultimately one unchanging essence underlies all the outer complexities and differences, especially amongst various societies and cultures, in humanity.

The Challenge of Opposites

From childbirth onwards we are exposed to the dynamic flux of opposites, and must make choices concerning them. Some will give us satisfaction and contentment, and others will cause us suffering and pain. We are constantly placed in this position of continually having to make choices, in order to allow for the growth of our faculty of reasoning.

Animals are not given this challenge. The cat, for example, does not have to cover itself with a blanket in order to keep itself warm in winter. We, on the other hand, must constantly strive to find the means of satisfying our basic needs of clothing, food and shelter, as well as an ever-growing number of other needs and desires.

The satisfaction of our needs, and the choices by which we attain that satisfaction, constitute our prime motivation. Together they spur the development of our faculty of reasoning and the understanding of cause and effect, and bring about our technological advancement. So nature, from the outset, drives us towards the development of our discriminatory capabilities through the necessity of having to make choices.

Wherever we look we are faced with opposites and we must make choices with regard to them.

One of the verses in the Qur'an describes the self as having been brought forth and, inspired, given the innate knowledge of what is virtuous and wholesome, and what is corrupt and decadent. The Qur'an indicates that the individual self is given the freedom to choose to follow the path of wholesomeness. The wise person actually has no choice but to accept the path of unity.

Attraction and Repulsion

The basic fundamental motivation behind all of our actions and behaviour is based on either the power of attraction or the power of repulsion. At all times, we find that our actions are based on attracting what we perceive will bring about harmony and equilibrium, whilst repulsing whatever we perceive to be the cause of disharmony and disequilibrium.

This constant flux of attraction and repulsion, of push and pull, is the essential dynamism upon which everything in this existence depends and is balanced. Even at a cellular level, an amoeba will move toward nourishment and away from a toxic solution.

At the physical level, our biological survival depends on our ability to pull in fresh air and push out stale air, and the same dynamism holds true at the emotional, intellectual and higher levels. On the emotional and psychological levels, we desire peace and tranquillity and repel anxiety and fear, whilst on the intellectual level we desire enlightenment through the attainment of knowledge and the repulsion of ignorance. Love and fear are two manifestations of the powers of attraction and repulsion. It is by love that we are propelled towards contentment and fulfilment and by fear that we avoid disturbances and undesirable things. The steady stream of life which, propelled by attraction and repulsion, is constantly balanced between harmony and peace and conflict and opposition.

Pleasure and Pain

At all times, we want to increase our experience of pleasure and contentment, and, conversely, reduce our experience of suffering and pain. Are experiences of joy and pleasure in this life representative of what is possible in the next consciousness or the hereafter? These experiences seem to act as tiny windows or glimpses into the inner state of pure bliss in another consciousness or life, that will be ours if we are properly prepared for it.

The same applies to our experiences of pain and wretchedness. These too are samples of what may occur by our own misdeeds if we do not follow the intended course of submission, surrender and responsible freedom during the training stage of this life.

From this point of view, every instance of pleasure or pain motivates us to move along a path which ultimately leads to a state where only infinite joy and no sorrow exists! Is this not the state in which Adam was originally created? Is this not reaching back to the real root of the matter?

Change and Non-Change

We emanated originally from a permanent or unchanging state, that prior to the act of creation. Change begins to take place at the point of conception. At birth, a child finds anything that changes outwardly to be disagreeable. The emergence from the womb itself is disagreeably shocking – hence the cry of the newborn which helps it to adjust.

As the child grows, it begins to think of change as something that is possible instantaneously, and it wants its desires to be satisfied, at once. As one matures further, one realises that outer satisfactions have no end and that the physical world offers little stability, whereas knowledge and wisdom are unending and provide a reliable, stable base. This process of awareness and change continues to the end of one's life, until the body is attracted back to its original source – the earth – and the self returns to its origin in an unknown dimension – the unseen.

The Quest for Freedom

Among the greatest dichotomies to which we are constantly exposed is our quest for freedom whilst simultaneously experiencing restriction. We know that whatever action we take, its outcome will be limited, be it in the sphere of material achievement, moral progress or any other arena. For example, although the athlete has the basic potential and relative freedom to achieve new levels or to set new records, his incremental achievement seems to get smaller with each successive attempt and appears to be approaching a point in which the upper limit cannot be stretched any further.

Whatever freedom an individual may think he has, it is still nevertheless bound within limits. Our life is confined within the limits of birth and death, and although we may enjoy a degree of flexibility, outer freedom is ultimately limited in this world.

Yet we are constantly seeking freedom by pushing to the furthest limits of our bounds. It is as though we are hearing an echo from deep within which reminds us of a boundless and limitless inner freedom which can only exist within our consciousness.

Freedom of No Choice

We are all bound by physically and materially limiting factors in this life. The human frame has its limiting capacities. Emotional and intellectual freedom also have their limitations. Absolute freedom we all know to be impossible, for even if we free our self from outer shocks and disturbances, we are not free from death. So how do we explain this drive towards freedom, and the underlying recognition and relativeness of freedom? Also, how can we arrive at the knowledge and understanding of this ultimate freedom whilst being bound within the framework of human reference? Is this not the freedom of no choice? Is it not true that we are continually searching for absolute freedom?

To embark upon the voyage of discovery in an ocean with no boundaries, we need the most reliable and best-designed of vessels. Recognising and knowing the limitations of our systems is the first step towards the journey of self-discovery. We have no choice but to seek ultimate freedom. This is only possible through self-awakening – from the limited to the limitless.

The Need for Security

As we have mentioned, we are all subject to opposites. We enjoy the experience of a jump or a free fall, but only if there is a secure base. We enjoy the dangers of a hunt – but only if there is a reliable home to which we may return, for hunting would be incomplete were it not for the base to which the prize could be brought back. Conversely, uninterrupted security would be unbearably dull. The security of a rock is not what we ultimately seek.

So at the physical level, we need the security of a healthy body, protective clothing and shelter. At the intellectual level, we need the security of knowledge. We need to be sure of the permanence of what we know. We want to be able to predict and be prepared. We shun disharmonious surprises. Even when we seek change, we wish to relate this change to a reliable base of known parameters.

Yet, even though we know full well that there is no absolute material or emotional security, we still strive after these unattainables. What is there within us that causes this paradox?

Basic Needs

At the outset of our journey in this life, we find that we share with our fellow human beings the desire for a sustained state of equilibrium – or as near to it as possible – in order to attain a state of contentment; and the basic needs of food, clothing and shelter have to be fulfilled before we can move on to attempt to satisfy our more subtle needs.

This is the reason why we are moved to sympathise with others who are afflicted with unfulfilled basic needs and the lack of basic essentials. This sympathy is a spontaneous acknowledgement and understanding of the basic position of discomfort or turmoil. This is why any appeal for aid to children or the aged, the helpless or the homeless, is generally responded to by every one of us. We all share this basic common denominator – there is no difference among us when it comes to the question of basic human needs, be they physical or emotional.

It can, therefore, be said that as long as there are people whose basic needs are not fulfilled, there will exist disequilibrium and what we often consider as injustice. As long as there is injustice, there will be agitation and turmoil preventing the possibility of a lasting peace. So all the political and utopian cries for peace are empty rhetoric as long as basic needs remain unattainable to people.

The Hierarchy of Fulfilment

There are priorities regarding the fulfilment of needs. Potentially it is relatively simple to fulfil basic material or physical needs, because they are subject to causal relationships. Therefore, filling an empty stomach is easier than obtaining mental tranquillity, and mental equilibrium is easier to achieve than intellectual fulfilment. Thus, people possessing material power seem to be better fulfilled in physical ways, but they still lack contentment in other, less material areas. They cannot buy what is missing in a shop – and they cannot get someone else to produce it for them. Total fulfilment still remains elusive.

We often find that people who make remarkable progress in the need-fulfilment hierarchy reach a point of desperation which makes them seek other means to further their progress, such as drugs or alcohol. Of course, these do not bring the fulfilment that is so desperately sought. They can only bring a short-lived relief from the drive for inner peace (whether mental, intellectual or spiritual) and harmony. Eventually, these people will come to despise themselves, because alcohol, drugs, and other artificial means disengage the natural dynamic process and bring about distortions and complications in their quest along the path of fulfilment.

It is the subtlest and highest of needs, then, which is the most elusive to fulfil and the object of the search for all of humanity. What, one may ask, is this ultimate fulfilment that we are all seeking?

The Drive to Achieve and Succeed

We constantly create objectives and goals in order subsequently to achieve and neutralise those objectives. This is a typically hyperbolic or cyclical exercise in the process of experiencing life. These attainments are not just ends in themselves. For there is a tremendous dynamism in the process of achieving the goal, and the individual develops a wider and deeper sense of connection with the environment, the community and the world. When one takes into consideration the whole of the environment, one is more likely to achieve and succeed, for he will have examined all the factors which interact upon the path towards the objective, and will have considered the peripheral and subtle elements that may impinge upon the target. The attainment of these considerations and viewpoints will no doubt bring about a sense of satisfaction and confidence, in addition to the actual achievement of the goal in question.

Therefore the achievement of goals also results in broadening one's vision and horizons. The closer one is connected to the dynamic interplay of the factors that surround one, the more likely one is to succeed in achieving the goals. This is why many of us are attracted to centres of decision-making and authority, to presidents and kings, for it enables us to anticipate the change of events in advance in order for us to adjust to the course of things in good time. Thus, it is useful for anyone setting up an enterprise to select partners who are connected with other networks – political, scientific, and so on that they may feed back into one's own system. In other words, the wider and more varied the individual's horizons and the quicker the input/output feedback, the more successful is that person in adjusting the direction of his efforts to achieve or alter selected targets.

Successes or achievements in themselves are only temporary resting places on the ever-spiralling stairway of human unfoldment. No sooner is one objective achieved than we set out again on the path in pursuit of yet another goal. It is a continual process in which we set up desires and then set about to satisfy them, and, by doing so, attain a state of neutrality which brings about harmony, equilibrium and peace of mind – which, together with neutrality, is what we all truly desire and love.

How, then, do we reconcile this paradox of love of achievement (i.e. the peace of mind attained by the satisfaction of desires) with the ever-continuing process of setting out yet again towards new goals and objectives? Why are we caught in this perpetual process of attaining peace, and then plunging once again into the unknown struggle?

A Prophetic tradition says that if you fill the biggest valleys in this world with gold and give them away, it will never satisfy the desires of any single man. So desires as such never end, nor will the continual struggle to attain them.

The Roots of Greed

Greed is often related to fear, instability and insecurity. If material accumulation and possessions could bring us security and happiness, then it would be only too easy to achieve happiness. Insecurity, however, can lead us to the discovery that physical or material possessions are not enough. This experience potentially could lead one towards progress and the discovery of an underlying inner security, which is the happiness we are truly seeking.

Are not greed and the material search, then, essentially perverted means of attempting to attain real security? Greed could be sublimated by our intellectual and experiential realisation that no outer accumulation will ever satisfy us fully. On the other hand, knowledge and experience of the inner life, and awakening to the higher spiritual dimensions, can propel us towards the one secure foundation behind all creation.

So the roots of greed and the power it engenders could be directed towards a positive end, once we discover the futility of greed itself and the desirability of true security.

Peace

We are driven in all circumstances to seek the tranquillity and equilibrium of peace. This is attained either in the form of static or motionless peace, such as in death or deep sleep, or in the dynamic peace of active life, and stability or equilibrium in changing situations. This stability or peace comes about by bringing together or connecting and linking unifying factors between diverse elements.

Peace comes about when agitations, desires and passions are calmed and settled, and a state of rest, equilibrium and contentment is attained. The body is biologically at peace when it is healthy, and at war when it is fighting a virus. The intellect is at peace when it has attained a certain understanding or perception, and has overcome a challenge of uncertainty and confusion.

Therefore whenever our peace is disturbed for whatever reason, we instinctively strive to regain that state of equilibrium; this, then, is the basic human drive which operates at all levels, physical, mental and intellectual, in all circumstances. One of the divine names of God is al-Salam, Peace.

Health and its Hierarchy

We need physical health in order to be aware of our body's need to attain equilibrium, so that the body and its mechanisms do not call our attention to it and distract us. Just as physical health means being in a state where there are no abnormal or disharmonious signals from the mind.

Generally, when we are in a state of disharmony or imbalance, an alarm goes off to call our attention to the problem in order that we may bring ourselves back to a state of contented harmony.

Once our body is in a satisfactory state, our attention goes towards mental health and well-being. The hierarchy of health moves from the physical to the mental and intellectual, and finally towards the higher and subtler spiritual realm. Though the relationships between these levels of health are strong, they are not easily definable.

In general, we seek steady overall health in order to move higher, into subtler degrees of awareness and well-being.

Man, the Unified Being

Every aspect of the human being and his behaviour, his desires, drives, expectations, actions, all follow a unific pattern of harmony and interconnection. If one becomes aware of the unifying process, then one experiences gatheredness, connectedness and harmony. If one is not aware of the overall pattern of the unifying force, then one's behaviour will be erratic and generally unstable. Invariably this undirected behaviour veers towards the edge of the intended path, bringing about experiences of disharmony, affliction, suffering and pain. Once off the path, destruction will be the inevitable result.

The bitter experiences of instability, disharmony and suffering are in fact a blessing, and an aspect of divine love. These experiences should be seen as guardrails on a highway, which will serve to bring one back to the centre of safety and equilibrium.

How else can the human being experience the opposites in this life unless he is actually subjected and exposed to them? So the human being experiences both the sweet and bitter, whilst an inner discriminative impulse within him recommends the sweet and repulses the bitter.

Man, then, already has nature's recommendation as to what to choose, but he must make the actual choice himself. The right choice will bring about the security of an original wholeness which is the hallmark of the unific, one absolute reality engulfing all manifest and non-manifest creation.

For the Love of Life

Even in adverse conditions, we hang on to life, the young and the old, rich and poor, ill and well. Indeed, the whole of humanity at all times and in all places desires to prolong life and to preserve it. Why do we do this? When we are unhappy or suffering in life, why do we wish to live long, even though we know that death is imminent? How can we reconcile these two opposite aspects, the certainty of death and the wish to avoid death?

One explanation of this paradox is that life on this earth has a purpose. Once that purpose is accomplished, the attitude toward death changes. The power of life is like that of light – its purpose is to enable us to witness and experience knowledge and enlightenment. Although enlightenment has a beginning, there seems to be no end to it. Like an aeroplane, once it is airborne, there seems to be no end to its possibilities. That is why no one with a sound mind will fritter life away.

Life's purpose is to rediscover our original unified nature. Whilst interacting in the transient world, the perfection and the beauty of this experience lies in our ability to fix or stop time. The urgency to discover the meaning of life is because of its slipping by.

All aspects of our basic nature relate to the condition of the primal adamic state, that is, to live in a true garden without concern or pressure of time – timeless bliss.

The Urge for Creativity

Our urge for creativity is similar in nature to our desire to proceed from the bounds of the known to the realm of the unknown. It is related to our intellectual and higher levels of expression.

If we ask a child or a simple minded person to create a painting, he or she will draw a house, a dog and a tree. The more evolved mind, however, rises beyond the limits of mere representation and thinks in terms of abstract ideas, beauty and other meaning. So creativity begins at the boundary where the world of the physical and the world of meaning meet, and moves beyond it.

We are characteristically drawn or driven by our creative urge, and it is in the creative act that we have the opportunity to exercise greater freedom than in other fields. Yet we find that we ourselves have been created without having been given a choice in the matter.

We are all the product of the natural creational process, and we too like to create. It is as though we are trying to participate in and echo the creational reality, or is it that we are trying to discover or follow the way of creation by imitating its method? Nature's beauty and creativity is boundless. Are we not trying to reflect the same truth of this endless beauty in our own creative expressions? One of the divine names of God is al-Jamal, The Beautiful. A Prophetic tradition says: Allah is beautiful and loves beauty.

The Drive for Knowledge

We generally associate fear, anxiety, enmity and distress with ignorance. Thus, we compare ignorance to darkness and knowledge to light. Essentially, we do not like darkness because it represents the unknown, and, as we have seen, we at all times wish to know. Our desire for knowledge is basic and elemental.

We want to know how to stop things which may harm, impoverish, deprive, or adversely affect us in any way. We equally want to know what enhances our fulfilment and well-being. We want to know how to move smoothly and speedily from the unpleasant and undesirable to the pleasant and desirable, from disequilibrium to equilibrium and from disharmony to harmony. We want to know how to be integrated in our approach and direction to things, rather than be confused by opposites, multiple choice, dualities and other uncertainties. We want to know how to choose from the many paths the best, safest, easiest, fastest and the most direct and effective one. Basically, we fear uncertainty and love certainty and reliability.

However, while we are in search of certainty, the cloud of uncertainty hangs over our heads. For example, while we seek certainty in life, the uncertainty of death and what follows it constantly haunts us. Yet this continuous crisis situation is the main source of constant opportunity for the wise.

At all times, we are matching new information and facts with past experiences, in order to add new dimensions to the ever expanding network of perceptions and knowledge which we are building. Our drive to expand this network increases with the increase of our knowledge. It is a never ending process. Each new level, stratum or dimension of knowledge opens new vistas for further search and assimilation, and the whole process is absorbing and obsessive because of the connective, integrating and unifying characteristic of its very nature.

Ignorance has the opposite effect; it is sterile, disruptive and limiting. Since this is contrary to man's nature, he is repulsed by its oppressiveness and darkness, and attracted to knowledge and light because it is connective, expansive and unifying.

Two Types of Knowledge

There are two types of knowledge available to man. One type is based on facts and information, is related to existential realities and deals with causality and that which governs the manifested existence of the objective world. This type of knowledge has its root in physical or outer reality. Let us call it factual and objective.

The second type of knowledge is more complex and is of a more permanent nature. This type of knowledge relates to higher or inner awareness and reality. For example, humanity has always honoured such values as courage, generosity and loyalty, and has always condemned their opposites – cowardice, selfishness and disloyalty. We have valued wisdom, patience and forbearance and abhorred stupidity and impatience.

Therefore, this subtler or higher type of knowledge, which we may term as primal, fundamental, or inner knowledge, is an integral part of man's consciousness, and is more developed in such individuals as prophets, realised beings, gnostics and others who have gained greater access to that inner awareness and fulfilment. This knowledge has its root within the human heart, and access to it is available only as a result of the quest for and unfolding of our inner inherently noble essence.

This inner knowledge belongs to a subtle, multidimensional network which is stimulated by external facts and information, causing it to receive and evaluate this data then respond in the most appropriate manner. So the greater the development of our innate knowledge, the more will we be able appropriately to absorb, coordinate, relate and utilise the factual knowledge and external information which comes to us.

Both kinds of knowledge are essential and complementary for human evolvement – the outer knowledge reflecting upon the network of inner knowledge to bring about a state of stability, reliability and harmony – even though we may still be acting dynamically in this world.

Prophetic traditions emphasise that there are two kinds of knowledge or science – one to do with existential realities and another to do with the path of awakening. The first concerns facts and information about the physical world, whilst the second is to do with guidance and illumination of the unseen, and the spiritual world.

Society, Culture, and Character

The development of the human self and its purification is essential to the establishment and maintenance of culture and civilisation. The building of a noble character and the acquisition of virtue are an integral part of the development and growth of individuals and societies. We can only survive, both as individuals and as a species, as a result of behaviour that is based on such stable noble character and virtue.

Just as a family is composed of individual beings, a society comprises an amalgamation of family units and its strengths and weaknesses are a direct result of the quality and cohesiveness of its values and goals.

A review of the lifespan and success of various societies, cultures and nations shows that the more vigorously practised are the higher values in a society, the stronger, healthier and more durable that society will be. We will invariably find that the society with the greatest strength is the one which most vigorously upholds the higher virtues, such as courage, generosity, loyalty, modesty, humility and honour. Conversely, whenever a society has become static and stops evolving, a state of decay sets in because the primal values have either been forgotten or at best only ritualistically observed.

The survival of a society in the long term, then, is dependent upon virtuous leadership and truly virtuous leadership is ultimately appropriate at all times and in all circumstances, for it can only result from such a developed character and awareness that transcends space and time.

Travel

Travel is always a reliable means of observing and acquiring knowledge of creation in this world.

There are two factors that give meaning to whatever we observe and experience during travel: one is change itself, and the other is the meaning of that change against a back-drop of reliable past knowledge. So there is outer movement and new experience, and there is also an inner, stable network of reference, against which the outer movement is measured and evaluated. What we are doing whenever we look at the customs and habits of different cultures is to try to discern the unifying factor behind the apparent outer differences. This is the true significance of travelling – we try to see the common denominator underlying apparent differences.

At first we may be confused, not understanding what we observe in a foreign culture. But when we relate this new observation to what we already know, this understanding connects the new information to existing past knowledge. The integration of new information brings fresh satisfaction and enrichment, unless we have simply shrugged it off and dismissed it with a value-judgement such as calling a culture primitive or ignorant, for example, in order to discard the perplexing or confusing observation from our system.

For we cannot accept confusion – we need unity and fusion for our peace of mind and contentment – and this is why we look for the unific network in everything.

The wider and deeper is our internal network of knowledge, the greater is the possibility of relating and understanding new facts and observations. That is why it is said that travelling broadens one's mind. It expands our knowledge, thereby reducing possible future shock due to unrelatable or confusing new input. We are constantly striving to expand our unifying network of understanding. We are enslaved to the quest of the ultimate, unific oneness.

The Qur'an enjoins upon us to travel throughout the land, seeking knowledge by contemplating the example of those who lived before us. They too were subject to good and bad and the affliction of constant change. Although they may have built the most stable homes, their final abode is no longer what they had planned. In the Muslim world, one will still find the shrines of many saints and martyrs, rarely those of kings and rulers.

Language

It is curious to note how language allows individuals of different origins to relate, connect and unite with one another. It is through language that we find that although people differ in colour or habits, they nevertheless resemble one another in the basic forces and powers that propel them to function. So language is a factor that takes apparent differences towards their root of basic sameness.

Another aspect of language is that it reflects the degree of evolvement and subtlety of a culture. Some languages are very pragmatically oriented, while others are not. Some accommodate conventional, human, existential requirements as well as the ability to communicate subtle and higher aspects which are not tangible or materially measurable.

Some languages are most suitable to communicate eternal or divinely revealed knowledge, such as Sanskrit, Aramaic or Arabic, while other languages, for example, are more adapted to conveying objective, scientific or technological information. Although most languages can also communicate the subtler aspects, ultimately, they are limited in their ability fully to communicate revealed knowledge, and that is why poetry and other forms (drawing and painting) of expressing the sublime often need to be utilised.

Religions

The purpose of divinely revealed knowledge and the Prophetic message was to reveal to humanity the most dependable and unchanging set of laws and codes of conduct, which would be in harmony with the natural and universal laws and realities. The Prophetic revelations describe man's life on earth as a process of growth and increase in knowledge and awareness, in order to prepare him for the next phase of experience, which is the state following the death of the senses. This state can be attained in exceptional cases purposefully and voluntarily in this life or commonly and involuntarily after the death of the body.

One of the original purposes of religion is to enable human beings to discover and practise the immutable, unchanging laws operating in the universe, whose origins are non-physical and which can be neither violated nor ignored. Human life is basically noble, and the essence of our being is of a subtle dimension to which we invariably aspire in order to experience the benefits that can accrue to us individually and to society as a whole. By following these guidelines, we are necessarily motivated towards a high degree of morality, thereby bringing about a state echoing that of the 'Garden of Eden' here on earth.

Nature has given us the choice of following its laws, and if they are followed, all will be in harmony. If they are not followed, we will find our existence to be disturbing, confusing, and ultimately intolerable, and we will have only achieved that disharmony and disunity in our life which we inherently dislike and abhor. Nature is always guiding us to avoid the self-created hell which we frequently bring upon ourselves and from which we suffer on this planet.

It can be said that the fundamental aim of all religions is to assist humanity to bring about a 'Garden' environment in our lifetime which we long for inwardly, and to strive towards security, safety, harmony and unity. That is the unified sublime state of the self which we are inherently programmed to attain.

The path of Islam (harmonious submission) was followed by all prophets and messengers throughout history. However, the laws of Islam as a code were completed by the Prophet Muhammad only fourteen hundred years ago. So all religions are in harmony and all prophets and messengers reflected the same truth and confirmed each other.

The Intended Destiny

As has been noted, humanity has a natural tendency to seek and understand ways that will lead to a lasting and harmonious state. The ultimate harmony comes about by the discovery of and adherence to the unchanging laws of nature, and by moulding our own individual direction and orientation to fit within those laws. Only then can conflict disappear, and our desires and wishes move in harmony with the original and ultimate purpose of creation.

The same rule applies to societies and nations. If the will of the individual, and the collective will of society, unify in that creational stream of universal laws, what emerges is a healthy society and community. The healthy society and community, in turn, sustain healthy individuals and help to rehabilitate the weak and the infirm. Thus, on both the personal and collective levels, we are subject to a universal current of dynamic interactions which, in turn, are then controlled by the multitudinal visible and invisible laws of nature. Nature's ways and direction in the long run will overcome the individual or collective desires and objectives, if they are in conflict. So it is only rational for us to know the universal laws of natural reality and the ultimate purpose of creation, and to work along with them rather than oppose them. Only then will we begin to see our intended destiny and the perfection of these universal laws.

Law and Justice

There are generally two sets of laws. The first is man-made and is based on convenience, prudence and expedience. When it is used to govern, it tends to be flexible and change-able, more often favouring the strong and the elite within the community, thus resulting in a basically unjust and oppres-sive system of governance. This set of laws is empirical, and is established according to man's convenience, changing from time to time and reflecting the current state of the peo-ple and their social values, as well as being greatly influenced by socio-economic factors.

The other set of laws is universal and does not change; it applies at all times. These laws have been revealed to human-ity through the highly evolved and awakened prophets, mes-sengers and gnostics, and are the body of laws which reflect and enhance the inherent values and virtues within us. These universal laws bring about lasting tranquillity and stability – and therefore justice and natural harmony in existence. They relate to our behaviour towards ourselves, towards other creatures and towards the source of all creation. Absolute justice is an attribute of the Creator, Allah, whose name is also al-'Adl, The Just.

The degree of success and durability of man-made laws, however, is related to how closely they approximate and reflect the universal laws. On many occasions we consciously attempt to reinforce the universal laws in our daily life, and it is often the difficulty of translating the universal law into actual specifics in our individual situation in life that is at the root of much of the trouble. It stands to reason, therefore, to conclude that the best universally revealed doctrine is that which goes into specific detail, in order to enable us to apply the laws and the spirit behind them successfully.

Morality, Virtue and Divine Law

All social systems throughout history show us that there are common norms and moral values which are regarded as good, and others which are regarded as bad. At all times, we find forms of behaviour which are considered acceptable and desirable and others which are not.

In most desirable and stable societies, as we have mentioned earlier, we find the higher virtues, such as courage, have always been held to be desirable traits, and the opposite, such as cowardice, have been considered undesirable.

Most of the basic virtues found in any one society tend to be very similar to those in other societies, and it is only their priority and the way those virtues are expressed that may differ. For example, in a society constantly facing external danger, we find that the virtue of courageous actions, physical strength and sacrifice are prized above all others, whereas in a society which is stable and agrarian, we find such virtues as modesty, temperance and kindness to be regarded as the qualities most valued.

Therefore it is not the concept of virtue itself that is in question; rather, it is what a society considers to be virtuous that changes. In another example, a society may attach great value and merit to the act of political imprisonment at a time when that society is undergoing a struggle for independence and freedom. The same act at another time, when the society is stable and in the hands of its own people, would be regarded as political agitation, being both undesirable and disruptive.

In order to understand properly the full meaning of virtues we need to understand the universally revealed laws. It is the revealed laws which show us the proper application of those virtues which arise spontaneously and naturally in the heart. Morality and virtue spring from the heart, but the way of conduct and behaviour must have its foundation in sound knowledge. The use of the intellect involves making choices and examining alternatives, and it is here that one finds that the prophetically revealed way is the optimum path and the most efficient means to achieving this objective.

We need to allow ourselves to be guided by the indications and proofs of the perfection of this prophetically revealed way in order to arrive at that which is already within us: the knowledge of right and wrong, and the morality inherent in our inner being.

The laws of the various revealed religious traditions have never contradicted one another. The laws and the message have always been the same. Rather, it was their emphasis and comprehensiveness which varied according to the extent of humanity's spiritual development and the state of its outer social form. When the ancient and slow-evolving Hindu spiritual teachings became increasingly ritualistic and socially oriented, Buddha arose with a teaching that strongly emphasised the development and awareness of the self and its psychology.

In a later age, the Prophet Jesus appeared at a time when the message of Moses had degenerated into a body of laws and regulations, crudely administered and abused by an elite group of religious custodians and through which the latter wielded great power over the masses. The emphasis of the teachings of Jesus was on the inner purification of the self and the renewal of the spirit of the law, in order to redress the imbalance which had occurred due to the crude application of the letter of the law.

However, the basic meaning and intent behind the law remained, and remain, universal and for all time. There was never any disagreement about the essence of the revelations brought by the prophets. All that differed were the rituals and practices of outer behaviour – whether, for example, the orientation for prayer would be towards Jerusalem, or Mecca, or elsewhere, or whether the day of rest should be on Saturday, Sunday or Friday. But there was never any disagreement that there should be a direction for prayer, or that one day out of the week would be set aside for rest and renewal.

True religious traditions are totally complementary to one another, in the sense that each succeeding religion added to and improved upon the previous one, until finally the basic code of conduct was completed and perfected for all humanity and for all time. It could be said that humanity had to evolve sufficiently in order to be able to adhere to the perfected and fully integrated body of revealed laws. The final result is a complete set of laws, by which we can conduct ourselves in life and arrive at a healthy inner and outer state, both individually and collectively. Without access to this divine code of conduct, we would be unable to progress successfully along the path of development and fulfilment. It is only through proper conduct that the moral values which are inherently pulsating within our heart will be able to manifest and bear fruit, in behavioural patterns which will in every circumstance offer us a safe and successful passage through this life.

Before we turn to our conception of the journey of the self, we need to establish an understanding of the basic nature and spectrum of the self. In the next chapter, we put forth a description of the self in all its aspects. For until the nature of the self is fully understood, there cannot be a proper understanding of individual or collective behaviour.

2

The Nature and Spectrum of the Self

Definition

In order to establish a clear foundation upon which we can develop our model of the self, we need first to define the 'self', *nafs*. The word *nafs* possesses many meanings and it may be defined as soul, or self, psyche, mind, spirit or life. It is also defined as a living creature, an animate being, essence, nature, inclination, appetite or desire, or personal identity. *Nafs* is derived from the root *nafasa*, whose root meanings include to be precious, valuable, or priceless, as well as, to compete or vie, to comfort or relieve, and to breathe, inhale and exhale. Other words derived from the same root mean a gem or precious thing (*nafisa*), a state of mind or mood (*nafsi*), mental attitude or disposition (*nafsiya*), breath, a swallow or gulp, and freedom or liberty (*nafas*), childbirth or delivery (*nifas*), psychology (*nafsaniya*); and the study of psychology is called *'ilm al-nafs*, the science of the self.

We shall define *nafs* as self or soul, which is non-physical, nor is it part of a body, nor is a physical body a necessary condition for its existence. The soul or self is that which breathes dynamism into physicality and gives it life.

The self manifests and evolves in this existence, in parallel with the growth and development of the body. Although it is not dependent upon the body for its existence, it exists and manifests in this life because of a body.

The nature of the self is indestructible and indivisible, and the fact that some part of us longs not to die echoes that immortal and eternal reality of the soul, or self. It emerged from non-time (pre-existence), lives in time, and returns to non-time (beyond physical existence).

The self has its origin in the realm of the unseen, and is primal and indestructible.

The self, or soul, then, is an essence which is immortal and non-physical, and which gives life to the physical body. It is influenced by the mind, will, intellect, heart and other cognitive processes.

The self unfolds and evolves in parallel with the growth and development of the human body, each moving towards its fullest potential. As the self moves towards growth of cognisance and awakening, the body moves towards physical maturity and, ultimately, decay and dissolution, back to the elements. Each therefore returns to its origin – the self, or soul, to its eternal non-time source in the unseen, and the body to the dust of the earth.

The self has been defined as 'a subtle, ethereal essence which carries the power of life, the senses, and all voluntary movement and action'.[1] It is the essence that illumines and vitalises the body. We could say that when the power or light of the self reaches all parts of the body, it is in full wakefulness. When the self disconnects with the outer or physical body but not with the inner, it is in a state of sleep, and when the self disconnects with both the outer body and the inner, it is called death. So sleep and death are of the same general nature, except that sleep involves partial disconnection and death involves total disconnection. We can liken the soul in relation to the body to that of light in relation to a lamp.

The *nafs* is also similarly defined[2] as that which is a body as far as its present existence is concerned, and a spirit (*ruh*) as far as its immortality is concerned. So the self comes into existence with the body, which is destructible, but its continuation after death is with the spirit (*ruh*), which is indestructible. It is stated in the Qur'an that 'the soul is one of the commands of [the] Lord' (17:85) and by this is meant that the soul has its origin not in earthly existence but in the eternal realm of the unseen.

The broadest usage of the word *nafs* in Islamic literature refers to the soul or spirit of the human being. In the writings of the Sufi masters, and in particular the treatises on self-knowledge and purification, the term was usually meant to indicate our lower nature and its baser impulses, as in the phrase, 'The continuing strife between man and his *nafs*'. The word *nafs* is frequently translated in such literature as the carnal soul which must be restrained and made patient.

Classifications of the Self

A basic system of classifying the self as consisting of three levels or aspects is described by many writers. The physician and philosopher Avicenna[3] describes these three levels in his *Canon of Medicine* as the vegetal self, the animal self and the rational self, and because of its usefulness, we will return to it in detail later.

Other writers have also followed a similar three-levelled categorisation in describing the self. Some have attributed to it three stations of being, or worlds of creation, but in all of these classifications, there are clear parallels which they share in common. These can be seen in the following classifications summarised below.

The Three Levels of Being

The three levels of being are described as the natural being (which is also referred to as the sensing being), the self-aware being, and the rational being. The natural being is regarded as the lowest level of the self, and consists of the physical aspects of the body and its mechanisms, including the entire spectrum of the outer senses, such as sight, sound, smell and so on. It is based on physicality and the senses which are in a state of constant decay (and eventually death).

The second level of being is called the self-aware being, and it contains the spectrum of the inner senses, such as imagination, memory, common sense and so on. It is an intermediary stage between the natural being and the next level of the rational self. Here, the self-aware being has access to the realm of imagery and ideas which are not based on physicality.

The third and highest level is the station of the rational being, and it is based on the intellect and the faculty of discrimination. The rational self contains the ultimate faculty of pure intellect, which is of the spirit and divine in origin, and its nature is permanent and eternal.

The Three Stations

Another classification of the three levels of the self is as the station of nature and the senses, the station of the self and the imagination, and the station of discrimination and divinity. Here again, the parallels with the other classifications are apparent.

The Three Creations

Similarly, further parallels can be drawn with another system of classifying the self, that of the three creations, or evolutions, of the self. The first creation manifests itself primarily through the outer senses of the natural, physical world. The second creation manifests primarily through the five inner senses of the world of imagination and non-physicality, whilst the manifestation of the third creation is by the power of the intellect and pure spirit.

The Three Worlds

We are given yet another categorisation, which is described as the three worlds of creation. The first creation is the world of nature and material phenomena with all its manifestations leading to decay and the process of recycling. The second creation is the world of images of the inner senses and the imagination, and this creation is without matter or physicality. The third creation is the world of images in the intellect, whose source is in the faculties of discrimination, differentiation and synthesis. The first creation unfolds into the second and ultimately leads to the third, and it is through these three stages of creation that the human self develops. Man, in truth, is a product and an evolution of these three levels of creation.

The Three Worlds of Pictures

A further classification describes the development of the self through a cycle of three worlds, and, again, parallels with the previous system are clearly seen. The first creation is the world of material pictures and is the realm of material events and occurrences. In this world of material pictures, man's natural sensing faculties develop from the outer senses that originate from his physical nature. This, therefore, is the world of the visible and the seen. Here, the existence of a picture – the 'idea' of a picture – cannot be separated from the matter out of which that picture emanated.

The second creation is the world of pictures of the imagination, and its source is the self. This creation is based on images and imagined pictures, which do not have their origin in matter. This creation is based on the five inner senses of imagination, memory, common sense and so on, and this therefore is the world of the unseen.

The final creation is the world of pictures of the intellect, and its source is man's faculty of reasoning and discrimination. It is the realm of higher understanding and awareness.

Summary

All of these classifications delineate a progression of the self in its upward journey towards completion and perfection. We notice that there is, in human nature, a forcible movement of inward purposefulness, whose ultimate goal seems to be the cognisance of the source, root or origin of man. We also note that for every inadequacy or incompleteness of the self, there is an innate and instinctive longing or drive for its completion towards a higher level. Once an inadequacy attains completion it identifies with it, and the new identity supersedes the previous one. So it is the nature of the self to be drawn towards its more noble and higher form and thus to its completion. In other words, within every ordinary self, there seems to lie a superself waiting to be born.

Classification of the Self According to Avicenna

As we have mentioned earlier, a basic classification of the self by Avicenna describes it as possessing three aspects which are referred to as the vegetal self, the animal self and the rational self. In life, the first matter that the self encounters concerns the act of feeding, which is followed by growth and development and eventually by reproduction. The next phase of the self is concerned with sensing and movement, and this is followed by the third phase of knowledge and discrimination. Within each of these phases there is an awareness of a perfection inherent within the self, which carries it towards its fullest potential.

The Vegetal Self

The vegetal self has three faculties or powers, namely the powers of feeding, growth and reproduction.

The first power is that of feeding which fashions an entity into one of its own species. The second is the power of growth itself, and that it grows in proportionate measure to its own kind. The third is that of reproduction and regeneration, which allows the vegetal self to reproduce itself through a seed, giving rise to a new cycle.

The Animal Self

The animal self has, in addition to the faculties of the vegetal self, the additional powers of comprehension and movement. The power of comprehension is to interpret and apprehend information from the outside world through the five inner senses (and we will elaborate on these later). The faculty of movement enables the entity to be able to transport itself according to its will. Although the vegetal self has a degree of mobility, its movement does not occur by will, since it is devoid of conscious will.

Mobility arises from two sources: the first is by the direct power of action, such as moving a limb or an appendage. This power is initiated in the nervous system of the body and transmitted through the muscles, thus causing the physical manifestation of movement. The second source is by the cause behind the action, that is, its intention. This primary motive has to do with yearning or desire. The motivation to move arises from the desire to obtain something that is wanted. This motivation in turn is based on the faculty of imagination, for when an image or a thought of what is desirable, or repulsive, occurs in the imagination, that image gives rise to a motive to move either forward or back, whereupon movement ensues.

So the animal self is drawn towards what the faculty of imagination deems to be desirable and necessary, and is repulsed by what it imagines to be undesirable and destructive, or by whatever prevents it from obtaining its desires.

This dynamic of attraction and repulsion is fundamental to all creation. The power of attraction and the power of repulsion are the two basic motivating factors in life, which we will examine in greater detail later. These powers may also be referred to as the powers of desire and anger, respectively, or the powers of push and pull.

The Rational Self

As the third and highest level of the self, the rational self possesses all the qualities of the vegetal self and the animal self, in addition to which it has the power of action, or doing, and the power of knowledge.

The power of action is that power by which the body is protected, nourished and raised to its full maturity, and by which the self is able to overcome the lower animalistic tendencies within itself.

As for the power of knowing, this is a power which can view matters and processes in theory and abstraction. It refers back constantly to the faculty of memory (which will be discussed later), by which it maintains its connection to the origin of all its actions.

So the journey of the self begins from the lowest stage of its vegetal aspect and evolves towards its highest stage until it reaches the objective for which it was created.

Further Comments on the Rational Self

The rational self, according to the thirteenth-century philosopher al-Tusi,[4] is the higher self, and, because its origin (that is, the origin of the self) is of the unified realm of the unseen, it always considers and judges in terms of unity because it is itself in unity and incapable of any division.

Al-Tusi also notes that, unlike the physical body, the rational self can contain all its different manifestations and attributes simultaneously. It can also perceive opposite conditions simultaneously, that is, it can comprehend both hot and cold, wet and dry, at the same time. It does not move from one state to another as the physical body does. The rational self instantaneously and simultaneously perceives all opposites and all potential states. It acts as a standard or reference point for change.

It is the rational self, therefore, that perceives all events that can be perceived through the senses at once and can judge them accordingly. For the rational self has within it a common denominator of sensing. It is called the unifying sense (we normally refer to it as common sense) because it has the ability to integrate at once all the various bits that it senses.

Furthermore, the rational self has the ability to reflect or weigh what it perceives outwardly against its own rationality and its previous experiences, and thereby to distinguish between the true and the false. For example, the sun appears as a small sphere in the sky, but the rational self knows that this is due to its distance from the perceiver, and that the sun is in fact many times larger than the earth itself.

The rational self is the abode of wisdom, knowledge and the higher virtues. It is designed to ride upon the animal self, which is the vehicle of the self to its higher virtues. The animal self ideally should submit itself totally to the rational self, like an animal that one can ride because it has been trained. If the animal self does not yield to the rational self, which is its rider, and instead follows its own whims and desires, then it will end up where it was originally – ungroomed, undisciplined, useless and in constant agitation, attempting to throw off the rider – without whom it will be doomed.

Whatever disciplinary measures are taken against the animal self by reason of its deviation from the will of the rational self (the parallel here being that of the rider who strikes his mount when it veers off the road that the rider wishes to pursue), the animal self visualises and pictures the agony and affliction of these corrective actions through the power of imagination. As for the rational self, it never left its high and noble abode from the outset – it has merely lent sentiency and the ability of imagination to the animal self.

The rational self has always been, and always is, in the abode of perfect bliss; its real nature relates to the divine. None of our earthly afflictions affects it.

As for the animal self, it can be happy or miserable according to the degree of its obedience to and harmony with the rational self. The animal self which has been in obedience with the guidance and wisdom of the rational self will find itself grazing in the pastures of the 'Garden'; while the animal self which has been obstinately rebellious and led by its whims, will find that it has led itself to the scorching agonies of the 'Fire'.

It is the faculty of comprehension and sentiency that informs the individual that he is at any point in an acceptably stable state or not. This matter is not dependent on the rational self as such. The rational self only lends the ability to comprehend. In proof of this, we observe that the person who is wounded or ill, whilst asleep, does not feel pain. The faculty that causes pain to be felt has turned its face from the world of witnessing to the world of the interspace of sleep. There is, therefore, no sentiency, and the patient feels no pain. In other words, once the rational self turns itself away, comprehension will no longer be present. Agony or pain, the sensation of goodness or joy, and so on, can only befall the animal self by grace of the rational self.

Abodes of the Self

According to the philosopher al-Miskawayh,[5] the centre and abode of the vegetal self is considered to be the organ of the liver, and is the seat from which it emanates. The basic nature of the vegetal self, as we have seen, is characterised by feeding, growth and reproduction, and among the chief functions of the liver are aiding the digestion and assimilating food. The secretions of the liver are also essential in the manufacture of certain hormones, including the reproductive hormones, and hence play a vital role in the powers of reproduction of the vegetal self.

The dwelling place of the animal self is the heart. It is in the heart that man's feelings, emotions and desires originate, that drive him on the one hand to pursue his lowest animalistic tendencies of appetites and anger, or on the other to rise to his nobler qualities of courage, modesty and other virtues.

The abode of the rational self is located in the brain, that part of the brain which is the master-centre of control and communication. All the higher mental abilities, including thinking, take place here.

The ultimate and highest self, which achieves the point of pure abstract comprehension and awareness, is linked to the spirit, and its nature is divine and of light.

The Senses and the Self

The development of the self is very much based on the development of both the outer and the inner senses. All of our senses are necessary for the growth and awakening of the self. However, they are needed only up to a point. After that, they can become a hindrance to our inner state of awakening unless the senses are utilised to serve the ongoing unfoldment of our inner, spiritual life.

In order that the self may comprehend and progress through its various stages, the senses in the first place are essential. They are of vital importance to the beginning and the early stages of the journey. They can be conceptualised as the vehicle one rides in order to reach a destination.

That is why it is said that he who loses a sense loses a door to knowledge. But once the self has reached its destination, and true reflection begins to take place (knowledge of the self by itself), the normal senses can then become a hindrance – unless, as we mentioned, they are properly controlled and utilised. For after consciousness, or awareness of a situation, comes the next state – pure consciousness or pure awareness.

The Five Outer Senses

The five outer senses are touch, taste, smell, hearing and sight. Of these, touch is the first and the coarsest of all the senses. It is physical sensation on the outer skin, and this sense is spread throughout the body. We can sense touch with any part of the body to varying degrees of sensitivity. We can sense heat and cold and comprehend whether something is hard or soft, coarse or smooth, heavy or light, wet or dry.

The sense of taste is the second in coarseness after touch. To taste is conditional upon being able to touch and have physical contact, but it also requires penetration into the tastebuds, assisted by moisture or saliva from the mouth. The senses work in close harmony, in that recognition of certain substances often requires the confirmation of more than one sense. To taste certain foods, for example, we often need the additional sense of smell. The more conditions needed for a sense to function, the subtler is that sense. So taste is subtler than touch because taste includes the condition of touch as well as others; and smell is subtler than taste, for it requires even more conditions.

The third outer sense is the sense of smell. In order to sense by smelling, molecules of a substance floating in the air must physically enter the nostrils and there penetrate the cells that have the capacity to assess them. So physical contact is still required, and thus it is considered with touch and taste to be among the relatively coarse senses because the condition of touch is necessary.

As a group, the senses of touch, taste and smell are the least subtle of the senses.

Hearing is the fourth sense, and it occurs when sound waves from the source of the sound reach mechanisms in the ear and cause these to vibrate. Although it is subtler than the previous three senses, hearing still requires a physical medium, such as air or water, to carry the sound waves. Sound, unlike sight, cannot pass through a vacuum.

Sight occurs when the reception cells in the brain respond to nerve impulses resulting from the action of light (photons) striking the eye. Light travels in a wave-like motion, and can pass through a vacuum. Unlike sound it does not require a physical medium, and therefore sight is considered to be the subtlest of the five senses.

The Five Inner Senses

The faculties of the five inner senses are the unifying sense, or common sense, imagination, the faculty of attributing meaning, memory, and the faculty of cognition or thinking.

The first and foremost of the inner senses is the unifying sense (*al-hiss al mushtarak*), and it is usually referred to as common sense. It is derived from the word *hiss* which means sense, and from the root of *mushtarak* (*sharaka*), which means to coordinate, share, combine or integrate, and also, to be the lowest common denominator.

The unifying, or common, sense is the faculty that allows us to relate and integrate the various precepts of the outer senses as well as the inner.

For example, the sensations perceived by the various senses, such as shape, colour, smell, texture, and so on, are coordinated in a coherent and meaningful manner – not by the eye, nose, or the hand itself, but by another sense altogether, which is the unifying or common sense.

The unifying sense also coordinates and integrates the images produced by our inner senses of the imagination, memory and so on, and thus it deals with the pictures of the inner world as well as the outer.

An analogy of the unifying sense in relation to the other senses is akin to that of a judge and his emissaries who bring him news and information from various sources. The judge organises these various precepts into a coherent whole and then makes a decision and acts according to the information supplied. The unifying sense, or common sense, then, is the single common denominator of all of the various senses.

The second of the inner senses is the faculty of imagination. The word *khayal* is an important term and its definition as imagination is much more comprehensive than its normal usage. It is firstly the capacity of producing mental images or of picturing in our minds a representation of a physical object when the object is not there. It is the conceptual ability to form images of physical reality even though that physical reality is not present.

Khayal is also defined as the ability to imagine forms composed of unrelated objects, such as an animal with the head of a man. *Khayal* also means apparition, fantasy, trace, dim reflection, or shadow. The root of the word is related to an attribute of the horse, for as the horse moves, its body reflects light and shadow as it undulates and shimmers in the sunlight.

The faculty of imagination also functions in our state of sleep, for we may hear extraordinary musical sounds, smell fragrances, or taste exotic foods. We apprehend these sensations by our imagination, even though there is no physical basis for their existence. We may conclude from this example that all of the qualities described, and others also, can exist in an abstract and absolute dimension in the absence of a direct physicality.

The imagination's capacity for picturing is not linked to or dependent upon physical reality. For this reason the imagination is sometimes called the inner camera. It has that capacity to preserve and store the pictures of the inner world. The imagination functions as a storehouse of its own inner pictures as well as of the pictures of the unifying, or common, sense.

There is yet another important feature of the faculty of imagination which is important to our understanding of the self, and it is linked to the concept we hold of the nature of reality. It is the *khayal* which is that faculty in the brain that perceives and experiences objects as solid.

When we undergo what is described as a transcendental or mystical experience (or an altered state of consciousness), we temporarily lose that faculty of solidifying objects. In that state, our experience of reality is profoundly changed and we no longer experience the everyday world as static and solid, even though everyone else around us does. It is that shared agreement that objects are solid that constitutes what is considered to be the real physical world. Our everyday experience of the real world, in fact, is only a limited spectrum of experience, just as sight is a limited zone of the total spectrum of light, and we are normally veiled from other than this limited zone. Many who have experienced mystical and transcendental states have described their experiences as though a veil had been lifted and their sight was temporarily clear.

Thus to be free of the *khayal* which locks us to the limited experience of everyday reality – yet to be able return at will – is a goal of the seeker of self-knowledge. That such a goal can indeed be achieved is attested to by the metaphysical, mystical and gnostic literature accumulated over the centuries, which is full of innumerable accounts of those who have experienced and described that vast other reality.

The third inner sense is the faculty of attributing meaning, *wahm*. *Wahm* is derived from the Arabic root, *wahama*, which means to imagine, suppose, surmise, presume, guess, fancy, believe, or to misconstrue or misinterpret. *Wahm* is frequently translated as illusion, and it can also mean delusion, erroneous impression, or conjecture. In our context, however, it is the positive sense of *wahm* that applies; and we shall define it as to attribute meaning.

The faculty of attributing meaning is the ability to comprehend that a person is a friend or a foe, that there is love or hate, friendship or enmity, between two people, and so on. Just as the faculty of imagination is the imaginative capacity of picturing, the faculty of attributing meaning is the imaginative capacity of understanding concepts in relation to people, situations or objects. It is this capacity that connects the intellect with the faculty of imagination, so the faculty of attributing meaning can be looked upon as an addition to the essence of the intellect.

An example of how this faculty works is shown first by means of our outer senses, when we see a person, and from the stored meanings in our memory bank (which is described below), we select by means of this faculty a picture of love, for example, which we associate with that person. Then by our unifying or common sense, we may arrive at a conclusion that love is not to be associated with that person at this particular moment, although we may also realise that the situation could change at any time. In this way, also, we develop complex discrimination and understanding.

The fourth inner sense is the faculty of memory (*hafidha*). The word *hafidha* is derived from the root *hafadha*, which means to keep safe, protect, remember or memorise. The faculty of memory acts as a depository or bank in which the pictures of attributed meanings are stored.

The memory stores the pictures of attributed meanings in the same way that the imagination stores the pictures of the unifying sense, as well as its own inner pictures of the imagination. The faculty of memory can bring back any picture of the past that it wants, provided that picture has not been erased.

The fifth inner sense is the faculty of cognition or thinking (*mufakirra*). The word *mufakirra* is derived from the root *fakkara*, which means to reflect, ponder, contemplate, consider, or to turn over in one's mind. The word *fikr*, also from the same root, is defined as the ordering of known matters in order to reach an unknown conclusion. *Fikr* is also extended to mean the transfer of the self from known areas that can be imagined or confirmed in the present, to as yet unknown areas or states that are potentially possible, based on what is already known.

The faculty of cognition is directly connected to the highest self which, as we have seen, is called the rational self. So this fifth inner sense, which is the cognitive or thinking ability, can only exist if the other four faculties already exist to support it. Thereupon cognition results as the outer manifestation of rationality.

The Relationship of the Senses to the Self

The self contains all the faculties of sensing, both the outer and the inner. It is the locus of the senses, but is not the senses themselves. The seer, after all, is not the eye, the hearer is not the ear, nor is the speaker the throat. It is man himself who is seeing, hearing and speaking.

The self that is within us is therefore the true origin and source of all the faculties of the outer and inner senses. It is the self that is the prime mover and motivation of all of these faculties.

The Relationship of the Body and the Self

First, let us consider this question: does the body sustain and carry the self, or does the self sustain the body?

A useful analogy here is that the body is like a sailing-ship, and the self is like the wind that drives it along. The ship itself cannot move unless the wind takes it (in whatever direction it will). Whenever the wind stops, the ship also necessarily stops. The same interaction occurs between the self and the body: when the self rests, or leaves the body, there is no life or movement.

The basic substance of the wind is completely different from the basic substance and quality of the ship. Similarly, the essence of the self is completely different from the essence of the body.

An interesting observation is made by the physician Avicenna, who says that when people see a magnet pulling at heavy pieces of iron, they are startled, but they are not surprised at how their self regulates and controls their bodies, drawing the body hither and thither, or how the animal self (the lower nature) draws them down from their ideals.

It is the self that dominates the body. The self carries the body, and it is the self that continues after the body dies. Our fear or dislike of death betrays the truth that so far as the self is concerned it never dies, but the body (whose nature is to return to its original elements) does.

The self and all of its faculties are independent of the body. Let us consider the power of the intellect. One of the proofs of the intellect's independence from the body is that, were that not so, one's intellect would always be of the same weakness or strength as the body – just as one's power of vision, for example, is related to the condition of the eye. We do not, however, find that clear or direct interdependency between the intellect and the body. There is no such relationship. One's intelligence does not normally wax and wane as the strength of the body does.

As far as the destiny of the body and its eventual death is concerned, there is a natural order of decay and death. Beside this natural destiny, we as individuals can interfere and bring about a quicker conclusion. An example is the neglect of one's health, which can cause the body to deteriorate more rapidly.

As in our earlier example of the ship, if the ship is maintained and looked after, there elapses a natural time for its decay and deterioration. But if it is not cared for or properly maintained, its natural destiny will be short lived and it will decay and fall apart more quickly.

Another way in which the 'ship' can be prematurely destroyed is if the wind blowing on it is of such magnitude or unpredictability that the ship cannot bear its force any longer. Similarly, if the physical and animalistic tendencies of the lower self blow upon the body to such an extent that it cannot readjust or repair the damage, a point may be reached where the body will finally succumb.

If the crew of the ship are men of knowledge, with an understanding of natural laws and measures, then when a hurricane hits the ship, their souls are in a tranquil and steady state. Such wise sailors would let themselves flow along the current in watchful awareness and knowing surrender. By their surrender – and here we are speaking of acceptance with knowledge, and not of fatalism – and by their patience and calm, their outcome will no doubt be the best possible under those circumstances. If the gales subside, then they emerge more experienced and strong, and if the ship is to sink, then even their departure was graceful and dignified. They meet their destiny in the next life with calmness and serenity.

The Spirit and the Self

The word *ruh* means spirit, and what it generally implies is the breath of life, or the origin of life. It is derived from the root *raha*, which means to animate or revive, to inhale or breathe, also to leave or to go away. *Ruh* has many usages, but we will primarily consider here its meaning in relation to the self.

The spirit is of the realm of the unitive source, that is, the unseen from which all creation manifests, and its nature is divine. It says in the Qur'an:

> And they ask you about the spirit [*ruh*]. Say, the *ruh* is one of the commands of my Lord and [about it] you are given aught of knowledge, but a little. (17:85)

The Qur'an informs us that the spirit is one of the commands or orders from the Lord. This command is defined in another verse, as:

> His command, when He intends anything, is only to say to it, Be! and it is. (36:81)

So the beingness or existence of anything comes about as a direct order or command from the Creator. It is when the spirit is breathed into human beings that they are given the power to subsist, exist and develop in this world, as it says in another verse:

> So when I have made him [Adam] complete and breathed into him of My spirit. (15:29)

So God blew of His spirit (*ruh*) into Adam, giving life to Adam's body. It is this same spirit that is breathed into Mary to bring forth the conception of her son Jesus, as is stated in another Qur'anic verse:

> We breathed into her of our *ruh*. (19:17)

In both these references, the *ruh* means the breath of life, the creation which belongs to the one reality.

We mentioned earlier that the spirit is a manifestation of the divine reality and, hence, upon death, it returns to its source in the realm of the unseen. It is related in one of the traditions that a close follower of the Prophet was asked,

'Where does the spirit go after it leaves the body?' The Prophet replied, 'Where does the light of the lamp go after the oil is used up?' What is meant here is that the essence of light is a constant or permanent state, and from it emanates various visible manifestations. When we put out a lamp and extinguish its light we have extinguished one of the light's modes or manifestations. It is as if the light of the lamp, like the spirit, has returned to its essence, or original state in the unseen.

To illustrate the relationship of the self to the spirit, we may use the following analogy of fire. If we think of fire as the divine Reality, then from it comes a spark which carries in it the nature of the fire entirely, and that spark is the spirit (*ruh*). When that spark ignites or touches upon a physical reality, it brings about a new manifestation, and that is the self (*nafs*).

So we can say that when the spirit conjoins with a physical entity (a human body), it results in the manifestation of the self. The spirit is often referred to as the higher self, whilst the self, which can experience the lower nature of man, is at the opposite end of the spectrum.

The aspect of spirit in each one of us is the same, whilst the aspect of the self varies from person to person and culture to culture. In our lower nature, we dwell in diversity and differentiation, each one of us with his different personality and fingerprint, each creating his own universe. As we move higher and evolve in our consciousness, we begin to transcend our physical differences and begin to see the similarities of motives and desires within us. The closer we are to the source of our origin, the fewer differences there are, while at the very source itself there are no differences at all. We are all in unity. This is what is meant by the one self, or the one reality.

Another description of the self and the spirit is that when the baser tendencies of the self are tethered, the spirit begins to emerge. As the tarnish on the self is polished away and purified, the presence of the spirit can manifest. So another way of looking at the self is that it is the place of the lower character that is to be risen above and transcended, and the spirit is the place of the higher character and virtues that one aspires towards. In general, the spirit always pertains to the subtler and higher element, whilst the self represents the lower aspect. Broadly speaking, this view holds through most of the teachings of Sufic literature.

The Heart and the Self

In order to illustrate the relationship of the self to the heart, we will first examine what is meant by the heart in the present context.

The Arabic word for heart (*qalb*) is derived from the root *qalaba*, which is to turn around or to revolve. This implies that the heart is functioning normally if it turns. If the heart is true to its nature, it will not be fixed or attached to anything. A sound heart can turn from any situation in which it is placed without resistance or suffering, if it is not pulled by or attached to that situation.

The implication is that natural creation intends for us to be related to, aware of and connected with whatever situation confronts us. Then, if it changes, one also changes. One's heart will turn. Ultimately and ideally, one's heart adheres to nothing and nothing adheres to it. There is only dynamic orientation, equilibrium and connectedness in flux – a primal, unific experience.

The analogy of radar is useful here. Radar, like the heart, transmits and receives signals. If it is fixed in one direction – for example, emotional attachment and possessiveness towards one's child – then should anything happen to the child, agony and pain will be the result. In addition, one's capacity to deal with the crisis situation, and thereby help others, diminishes, defeating one of the main objectives of love (care, concern and service). But if one's heart were unattached and freely scanning the entire field, the affliction would have been put in the right perspective and not caused such deep or lasting suffering, and thereby the outcome would have been handled more objectively and effectively. Obviously, we all have attachments and expectations in this world and it seems we cannot exist without them. However, we are speaking here of the degree of attachment and our expectations from it.

In Sufic literature, the heart is often defined and considered as a divine subtlety attached to the physical organ of the heart, and it is that subtlety which holds the truth within man.

The heart is also the originator of all our feelings, emotions, appetites and desires. It is also the dwelling place of the animal self and hence it is where the powers of attraction and repulsion emanate from.

One viewpoint[6] defines the heart as the whole power behind the human being, both the self and the spirit. In this point of view, the heart is equated with both the self and the spirit.

Another view prefers to relate and connect all cognisances and understanding to the heart, implying that the brain relates to the heart. Comprehension and understanding then are directly related to the heart. The brain is only a further means or auxiliary by which comprehension takes place. This view pinpointing the heart as the centre of cognisances is supported and confirmed by the reference in the Qur'an which says:

> Have they not travelled in the land so that they should have hearts with which to understand, or ears with which to hear? For surely, it is not the eyes that are blind, but blind are the hearts which are in the breasts. (22:46)

The Heart as a Battlefield

The heart has also been described as the battleground of the intellect and the self. In order for the self to move away from its lower nature, it requires the light of the intellect and discrimination to show it the proper nourishment and fuel that it needs, in order to evolve towards its higher self. For the self and its body need to dispel from it whatever causes it harm and deflects it from its natural course of progress, and to attract to it whatever is conducive to its evolution.

The source of the two powers of attraction and repulsion dwell in the heart, and these forces can be looked upon as two armies of soldiers.

The army of the power of attraction, or desire, has an inner and outer aspect. The inner includes all urges and desires, such as hunger pangs and other needs, as well as the desire for intangible goals such as companionship or status. Its outer aspect is to do with the body itself, and its actual ability to bring the food to it and to achieve its other outer goals.

The other army is the power of repulsion, or anger as it is often referred to. Its inner aspect is anger against what we dislike (and we usually dislike anything that prevents us from satisfying our desires). Its outer aspect is again the body itself and its limbs, by which it repels that which is undesirable.

If these armies of attraction and repulsion are left to run rampant by the animal self, they will indulge themselves in the base tendencies of its lower nature.

So the heart calls upon another and loyal army, which is the intellect and discrimination. Its soldiers are knowledge, wisdom and reflection. It is the intellect which sheds the light of discrimination which will ensure that what we pursue and what we turn away from are conducive to our growth. This ability to discriminate functions like a spy constantly ensuring that there is a feedback mechanism, and that we take the right course.

If we call upon the army of the intellect, we can ensure that rebelliousness and transgression will not take place. But if we neglect our knowledge and wisdom, and allow the army of the powers of anger and desire too run rampant, the result will be total destruction. If the soldiers of anger and desire are subdued, they will help and guide one along a safe passage, becoming the best of companions on the way. Here the heart is considered the same as the rational self, because the heart, as we have mentioned earlier, is a clear reflector of the truth behind man.

The Intellect and the Self

The Arabic word for intellect is *'aql*, and is derived from the root, *'aqala*, which means to be endowed with reason, to possess intelligence, to comprehend, to understand.

The intellect, in its highest sense, is a sublime power which receives the unveilings of pure light. In its lowest sense, it is the power of ordinary reasoning.

The intellect is said to perceive things in their reality. Its uniqueness is that part of it can become the whole (like a hologram, which will be discussed in a later chapter).

It is also said that the intellect is the vice-regent of the divine in human beings. It calls us to be united with the First Cause. Our intellect thinks of the First Cause as most noble and perfect, and deems it its duty to attain its divine attributes and qualities. Without the intellect, or the faculty of discrimination, there would be no enlightenment.

The intellect is a source of power for the rational self, though they are not identical. The self is always the doer and the intellect is only one of its instruments. The intellect obeys the self in the way that the knife obeys the hand. Hence, the more conscious and aware is the self, the more sublime is the purpose to which the intellect can be applied toward the higher development of the self. The great master Ali ibn Abi Talib[7] says that the intellect is a sword, so use it to cut down your whims and desires.

The intellect comes from the realm of absolute Reality, and by its light appear the forms of all things knowable. The images and the experiences which we perceive by the intellect have their own reality, in the same way that an image we perceive of the outer world of the senses has its reality. In fact, the images of the intellect have a greater reality than the images of the outer world which we consider to be real. For the material world is only a shadow of the world of the intellect, which is pure light – the reverse of what is normally considered to be true.

That is, in fact, the meaning of another saying of the master, Ali ibn Abi Talib: 'And in you is folded up the cosmos'. By this he meant that the reality of the world within our intellect and our self is far greater in truth than the world we witness outside ourselves. It is as though the self was brought into this world to become accustomed to its shadows, in order to be prepared to witness the hidden yet dazzling reality. It is stated in the Qur'an, 'Thus do We [i.e. Reality] make the signs clear for the people of intellect' (30:28).

In summary, we may glean further insight into the relationship between the self and the intellect in the word 'iqal, which is derived from the same root for intellect. 'Iqal is the cord used for hobbling the legs of the camel, preventing it from going astray by subduing and controlling it. This is also what reason does to man. Another meaning of 'iqal is the looped rope used to secure in place the headcovering used by Arab men in the Middle East, implying to contain and tether oneself by subjugating the self to the faculty of reasoning and intellect.

Summary of the Self to the Spirit, Heart and Intellect

It has already been said that the self has been formed by reason of the descent of the spirit – that divine spark from the unseen – into physicality in the world of creation. So there is an affinity and love between the spirit and the self in the same way that there is an affinity and love between Adam and Eve. At the time that Adam descended and dwelt with Eve, the spirit descended into earthly physicality and the self was formed. The spirit, then, dwelt with the earthly nature and caused it to be a self. As a result of the dwelling of the spirit in the self, the heart emerged. What is meant here is not the physical heart, but the subtle heart, which we described earlier.

To say that the heart comes from the union of the spirit and the self from the world of the unseen, is the same as saying that offspring come from the union of Adam and Eve in the world of creation. If it were not for the union of the two – that is, the spirit and the self – the heart would not have come about.

As the spirit aspires towards its origin in the unseen, the heart will yearn towards the spirit, like a faithful and loyal son' to its father. In the same way, the self will yearn towards the heart, like a loving and compassionate mother towards her son. Thus, if the self yearns towards the heart, it will lift itself above the material world and its faculties will be oriented in a higher direction. It will gradually find the aspects of worldly existence of diminishing interest. If, on the other hand, the self takes entirely to its lower nature, it will dwell only in its lower, materialistic tendencies and appetites.

In summary, then, we have seen that in order for the self to move away from its lower nature and overcome it, it requires the light of the intellect and discrimination to repulse what is harmful to it and to attract what is conducive to its evolvement. For it is by the intellect in its highest sense that enlightenment can be attained.

3

The Journey of the Self

We intend to introduce a simple yet complete outline of the journey of creation and the parallel journey of the self, their emergence, development, sustenance, their growth toward highest potential, and subsequent decline. The journey consists of five distinct yet connected phases, which complete the cycle of the journey of the integrated self. Each phase is dependent upon, and a product of, the previous phase. Each phase unfolds into the next one.

The journey of the self as we mentioned earlier is based on a pattern that charts a parallel progression of the outer (biological) and inner (conscious) development of the human being. The journey focuses on the microcosm of the human being, although the stages of development are echoed in the macrocosm of the universe. These phases are meant to be seen as a general guideline of human development and, as such, there will necessarily be overlapping. Also aspects of earlier phases to varying degrees of intensity will remain active throughout one's life, even as one progresses in one's journey.

In this chapter, the demarcation of phases by age is intended to be seen as general and qualitative, rather than specific and quantitative. The phases will overlap, one to the next, but the overall pattern, however, is one that has its own validity. We also must remember that for every rule there is an exception, and that exception only serves to prove the rule. But the exceptions are few and far between.

Phase One: The World of Absolute Unitive Reality

The phases of the creation and development of the human self can be described in parallel with the description of natural creation as a whole, that is, the creation of the cosmos itself.

Prior to the occurrence of creation, there was non-creation or non-manifestation. There was no movement prior to the emergence of the discernible energies and events of creation. There was total silence, an indescribable dimension, the realm of the infinite void. It was the primal, indivisible world of the absolute unmanifest, a non-space-time zone, not subject to the physical or natural laws experienced in time. It was a totally different domain, one that we cannot even imagine. It was a world of pure and unific consciousness. It was the world of absolute zero and infinity in all aspects.

The eternal void was an infinite, boundless ocean without waves or movement, from which, however, creational waves and movement emerged.

So from the unmanifest emerged the manifest physical worlds. From the unseen the visible and experiential made their appearance to be witnessed by creation itself. All creation originates from that reality of unific eternal quietude.

Absolute reality was completely dependent upon itself as it always is but in total unity with no manifest duality. This state of reality existed prior to the creation of matter. 'I' in that phase was unknown. There was no one to reflect or talk about it. This phase is the absolute world of the unseen: total stillness, total unific equilibrium, and stability.

From the world of the unseen came the command, 'Be!' However one conceptualises this event, it happened. Creation began. There is a good description in the Qur'an of the story of creation. It tells of the inception and creation of the cosmos and the worlds of celestial and terrestrial creation, the rise of consciousness and the subsequent confrontation of good and evil, obedience and disobedience, and the development of the macrocosm and the microself.[1]

We cannot really conceptualise the full state of creation, the actual emergence of duality, of cause and effect, nor even imagine that absolute state of peace and contentment from which we emerged. We cannot, while functioning in this world of time, imagine a state of non-time. We can only go back in our insight up to a certain point – and then give up. Imagination itself is a faculty created by the timeless reality – how then can it comprehend its own cause?

We can conceive a measure of infinity in terms of the speed of light. What might lie beyond that so-called infinity is no longer perceivable or conceivable by us. Any concept of it is beyond our system's bounds. We have moved into another dimension, another frame of reference entirely, and that is the zone of the unseen.

Reality willed our present universe, Be! – and creation began. Its equivalent on the human level is the emergence of the light of consciousness. At that point, all that the microself – you and I and everyone else – knew was its own essence, by itself.

At that point, then, from the realm of the unseen emerges the spark of creation, seen and bounded. From the formless void of the cosmos came the first shattering explosion of the Big Bang, as some scientists call it. In the dark void of the human womb comes the emergence of the light of consciousness. These different manifestations are descriptions of the same event, for the human (microself) reflects the heavenly (macrocosm), and the terrestrial echoes the celestial. In the Qur'an it says:

> We shall show them Our signs in the universe and in themselves until it becomes clear to them that it is the truth. (41:53)

The Qur'an also challenges us to accept the fact that there existed an absolute unific state before the act of creation, and asks:

> Was there not a period of time that came upon man when he could not be mentioned? (76:1)

The challenge is for us to seek an answer within ourselves. How, after all, could something come from nothing, then again vanish into apparent oblivion? The meaning here is that man's existence was known, or decreed, but in another frame of reference altogether – in the system of the unseen, in the timeless, limitless, eternal book, whose faint echo and copy appears in the flimsy world of material and physical reality.

In describing the journey of the self, it is essential that we understand that this phase did exist. We cannot, of course, prove it except by extrapolating and postulating. The fact that we all search for our roots, tribal or cosmic, is a proof of our longing to confirm the unific network in time and beyond. With this assumption made, we will come to the postulatory evidence in the pages that follow.

Phase Two: The World of Inner Dependence

The earliest stage of creation that the Qur'an mentions is the emergence of the cosmos. In that gaseous state, the two aspects of creation, heaven and earth, were connected. Then they drifted and were split apart along a certain prescribed pattern. The Qur'anic statement suggests that this separation was designed, destined and already predetermined. In this way creation occurred, and duality was manifested as heaven and earth, liquid and solid, hot and cold, and so on.

With time, the different systems – celestial, terrestrial and human – began evolving on scheduled courses. They unfolded in stages following a process of inner programming from inception to maturation. This second phase is what we shall call the world of Inner Dependence.

In the same way that the outer cosmos has its own built-in laws which cause it to expand and develop, the human child, the microself, once conceived, will also develop through its own built-in unfolding. The mother has little to say in this process and once the inner unfolding has begun, it takes over. There is an inner dependence of the foetus (microself) upon its own innate primal laws. Both macrocosm and microcosm are dependent on a separate inner life of their own that directs their course of unfolding during this phase of Inner Dependence.

Astrophysicists tell us that a great deal occurred in the

first few seconds after the cosmic Big Bang occurred. Then in the millions of years that followed, much less happened in comparison with those first few seconds. In other words, the initial brief stage was far more momentous and many more events took place. That initial stage of a few seconds was effectively equivalent to the millions of years of unfoldment that followed.

The same situation is substantially true of the inception and creation of the human being. We observe that the development of the embryo in the womb immediately after its conception is rapid. Within the first few weeks of life it is virtually formed and the remaining months of its life in the womb are a process of gradual completion of its development.

During this phase of Inner Dependence, the identity and the individualisation of the cosmos and of the foetus begin to occur. Millions of years in the life of the cosmos passed before specific and separate identity and individualisation occurred, in terms of planets and stars and the formation of galaxies. Prior to this, the cosmos was a fiery, gaseous oven of incredible heat, forming the initial celestial bodies and different galactic systems within it. For the microself, the foetus, this phase is the nine-month period in the enclosure of the womb until the human being is physically formed.

In this period, as far as the microself is concerned, the vegetal self is developed and is operative. The foetus grows and unfolds like a plant in nature. It grows and nourishes itself in an ecology of limited mobility. Its state in the womb parallels the situation occurring outwardly on the earth. The first life that appeared on earth was likewise tiny bacteria and the simple vegetative organisms.

In phase one, then, there is a boundless and limitless unitive reality whose system is total Self Dependence. In phase two, we have a system of Inner Dependence, which is wrapped in itself, unfolding by itself, and growing towards the next phase of Outer Dependence.

Phase Three: The World of Outer Dependence

The beginning of phase three is the manifestation of the definable and discernible heavens and earth. For the microself, this phase is the pain and agony of individualisation which starts at birth. This stage heralds another release, another unfoldment. The birth of the child comes with a cry.

In phase three, then, the child is born. The wet, infirm being emerges from the womb to live off the breast of the biological mother. Slowly, it learns to feed from mother earth. The duration of most formative learning in this stage of Outer Dependence generally covers the first seven years or so of life. Outer dependence in the general sense, however, continues all one's life.

In cosmic terms, the earth is born and cooled off from the cosmic furnace. Land and sea separate. The water cycles cool the earth and create the water channels like veins of the body. After the individual elements assert themselves and mineral life is formed, vegetative life develops. Primal simple life and later animals begin to roam about. Birth, the dawn of creation, and the development of complex life from simple unitary cells.

During this state, the physical and material forces grow and prevail with maximum force. In the case of the cosmos, we have witnessed the awesome power of physical matter in the sudden emergence and eruption of fire and rocks on earth, the ever increasing number of planets and the galactic systems, together with the built-in physical laws that hold and bind them. The mass of planetary bodies and their energies exhibit an awesome majesty and beauty.

The same forces and processes prevail in the microself. The material and physical needs and forces in the child prevail. The physical body asserts itself, demanding food, satisfaction, health, peace, tranquillity and equilibrium for the body. The first motherly action when the child is born is to reassure it and put it to the breast.

The earth, too, once it is born, is cooled and energised by the rain. The water cycle, seasonal cycles and an incredibly vast mosaic of outer sun and planetary bodies, dependence and interdependence begins.

In this state, the vegetal self is predominant in the life of the newborn. It possesses three powers – those of feeding, growth and expulsion. These systems develop in complexity and are refined as the child matures. The newborn is totally concerned with preserving its body through attracting and obtaining adequate comfort and nourishment. The appetites and instincts of the child are now clearly manifest. The other activity of the child is the repulsion of whatever is harmful to its body: automatically, by the expulsion of its own wastes, and consciously, by repulsing what it dislikes – milk which is too hot or too cold, for example. If the two processes of attraction and repulsion are not functioning properly, the balance is disturbed and the child will grow ill. The physical body has within it the mechanisms and controls which determine its state of comfort and equilibrium (good) or disturbance and discomfort (bad).

As the child develops and takes on the qualities of the animal self, it acquires in addition two other powers – of movement and that of comprehension.

The child now has emerged from the safe environment of the womb, where it was protected, contained and sustained. The child in the womb was not aware of its environment, or indeed of its own life or its mother. Now, suddenly, the child is dependent on the breast and has an inherent sense that if that dependency is discontinued, it will suffer. Its concern and anxiety concentrates primarily on feeding and other related basic activities of the animal self. Outer dependence is recognised.

The created stars and macrocosm continue on their

journey of growth and expansion without the consciousness
or awareness of their relationship or dependence on the
celestial bodies. The earth is unaware of its dependence on
the sun and the sun in turn on the solar system, and so on.
The macrocosm is simply in programmed submission to the
celestial creational forces, whereas the microself emerges
with a degree of basic conscious awareness, the foundation
of its intellect, and finally, later on, sublime awakening.

During this phase of Outer Dependence, the next phase
of Interdependence begins to take root, as the outer and the
inner begin to interact and relate. Here, also, the experience
of opposites begins to emerge firmly. The child is dependent
on the mother, the mother is dependent on the father, and
the father and the family unit in turn are dependent on
society, and so on. Each unit is dependent upon a larger
or more secure unit. Ultimately, the microself system is
dependent on the macrocosm, and the macrocosm seems to
be created for the convenience of the microcosm. A pattern
of Outer Dependence predominating in the child has clearly
begun to emerge.

The power of interdependence and connectedness is
such that each new star born affects the entire cosmos, just
as each child affects the entire household, the whole society
and ultimately all humanity, although most imperceptibly.
Should the child be a modern Napoleon, or preferably, an
enlightened leader, its influence on the entire world will
be noticeable. Whenever a new energy manifests from the
unseen, whether in the form of a star or a child, the pattern of
universal adjustment, absorption and influence repeats itself,
for every ripple in the pond affects the entire pond and its
microsystems.

However, there is another viewpoint by which we recognise the specific identity and self-containedness of the entity.
Every star is, so to speak, enveloped in itself, and reflects a
measure of completeness, independence, assertiveness and
uniqueness, with its own spectrum of radiation and its own
centre of gravity, and other individual characteristics. Yet,
like a hologram, each star reflects the characteristics of the
original total cosmic model.

Every child is also self-centred, and sees (or at least asserts)
itself as the centre of the universe, which is, practically
speaking, its world. In this sense, every child sometimes

behaves like a despotic tyrant. It wishes for the entire creation to revolve around, support and pamper it. Let a three-year-old child be the centre of attention and see how complex his performance will be, and how content he becomes by commanding attention and admiration.

During the early period of development of Outer Dependence, the child fully recognises that it is totally dependent on the world outside. The child's behaviour and attention then focus upon this new multidimensional umbilical cord, which grows in complexity.

The span of the early stage of the child's unique mother-dependence is generally the duration up to the time it is weaned. In Islamic tradition, this period is considered to be two years from birth. During this time, the child recognises, accepts and lives with the fact that it is completely and utterly dependent on its mother (or her equivalent). But towards the end of the period of weaning, he broadens and transfers that dependence, at least partly, from the mother to other sources of nourishment and means of fulfilment, such as other family members, the refrigerator and so on.

So the phase of Outer Dependence expands and develops in an ever-widening circle. The first dependence is on the breast. Later, the world replaces the breast.

The Seven Factors of Influence on the Self

There are seven major factors that exert considerable influence upon the life of every person and they can be described as follows:

1. *Conception.* The circumstances, conditions and state of the parents at the time of conception of the child is one such factor. The relationship between the mother and the father, the depth and nature of their love, trust, understanding and all other related points between them will reflect to varying degrees at a subtler level upon the child.

2. *The genetic factor.* The genetic heritage of the child, which it inherits from both its parents, bears considerable influence upon the life of the child, often irreversibly in one direction or another. These inherited characteristics or states can be physical, and can appear at birth or more subtly at deeper levels at a later stage in life.

3. *During pregnancy*. The condition and state of the mother during the nine months of pregnancy influence the child in more ways than simply by the quality of its food intake. The inner state of the mother – stability, security, confidence, love, optimism and so on – and the conditions of her environment, quality of food and rest are also of great importance.

4. *Conditions at birth*. The physical environment at the time of delivery is a factor of influence. Glaring lights and an indifferent hospital staff are bound to increase and intensify the trauma and shock of coming into this world. In contrast, being surrounded by loved ones in a room with a gentle ambience and the genuine concern of family members offers a better welcome for the sensitive newborn. It is a well-known fact that children born in a well-prepared and pleasant home environment are given an easier start in life and a stability which will influence them later on.

The actual time of birth also reflects upon the relationship between the macrocosm and the microcosm. As we have observed throughout this cycle of the self, there is always a clear parallel development between the greater cosmos and the microcosm, and the state of the cosmic realm is somewhat reflected in the microself. The position of the stars and planets and the general cosmic state does relate to the personal cosmology. This is why some astrologers can predict with a degree of accuracy the orientation and tendencies of a child if given the exact time and location of its birth. Other factors however may be more decisive and could overshadow the influence of the cosmic condition, but one cannot deny the fact that the heavenly bodies do exert an influence on the general predisposition of the individual, with particular reference to strong and weak points in the physical state as well as character.

5. *The weaning period*. The fifth factor is the growth of the child in its first two years of life. The material and the emotional quality of the food and nourishment it receives, the attention and love of the parents (or the absence of these), all exert their influence. The environmental, social, material and other conditions of the family are also extremely important during this stage of life. Naturally, the healthier and happier the parents are, the more likely it is that the child will benefit, other factors being equal. These formative years leave their

indelible mark on the child and are reflected most prominently in the mental and emotional state and tendencies of the person later in life.

6. *The first seven years*. During this period, the child develops and exercises his senses and other faculties by increased interaction with the outer world, and the animal self becomes pronounced and developed. The subtler cognitive faculties also begin to evolve. With these, the child has the ability to distinguish between what is acceptable and what is unacceptable, and between right and wrong according to the values of its family and others with whom it interacts. Its powers of reasoning, however, are still flexible and underdeveloped. By the age of about seven, generally speaking, a healthy child is ready for appropriate instruction, education and grooming – a sound clean tape upon which can be etched and recorded a desirable track.

7. *Personal will and determination*. This factor is of considerable importance and has much to do with the innate, primal, inner and spiritual aspects. If all of the previous six factors have elements that weaken or work against the individual, the seventh factor can still predominate and overcome some of the limitations and enable the person to attain spiritual awakening. No doubt all the previous factors come into play to varying degrees at all times, but if the individual is determined to gain access to inner knowledge and light, his success will depend to a great extent on his determination to awaken, and to adhere to and follow a real teaching and a path of conduct.

The seven factors described above constitute the major influences at work on the destiny of the individual in general and broad terms. They have been presented as an illustration of milestones in one's life.

Summary

We have observed in this third phase of Outer Dependence that the self begins to mature and the individual grows and strengthens physically.

At the end of its first two years the child has generally been weaned from the breast, but it is not weaned from dependence on specific adults. It is still completely dependent on others for clothing, shelter and other needs. This limitation, dependence and need, imposed by nature upon the child during this period, acts as a spur for the faculty of reasoning and intellect to grow and develop. The cat is born with its fur coat to protect it against the elements, but man must make arrangements for food, clothing and shelter. It is these basic needs that stimulate our minds by interacting with the world. Our very limitations, basic needs and deprivations speed up the development of our creative thinking and intellect as we strive to attain efficient physical (both in body and environment) harmony with the elements in the outer world.

The child loves its parents because of the familiarity, interaction and support which bring balance and tranquillity to the child, but at the same time, it yearns to have its own store of food. This is a desire for independent security. It may seem greedy for the child to hoard, but this is in reality a reflection of its inner desire for self-reliance by securing additional insurance of a source material and physical security.

During its first seven years, the child begins to broaden its horizons and sees more and more that the limits of its environment constantly expand and extend further.

With this broadening of horizons come new unknowns and surprises, with the attendant agonies and joys of growing awareness. Each time the child is surprised by a new experience, the input or stimulus is processed into the system and related to what is already there. So consciousness and intellect continue to broaden and deepen, providing a more coherent and stabilising foundation for new experiences to be related, processed and absorbed into the network of knowledge already there.

As the child increases in its interaction with others (peers and adults), its new experiences will beget a certain value of acceptability or rejection. It soon learns that certain behaviour or action brings about a beneficial effect (good feeling and reward from others). Obedience to the system of values in society will also ensure acceptability and, thereby, the satisfaction of future needs. One learns to give in order to get and appreciate the balance and equilibrium that comes from such cooperation and exchanges. So starts the rise of ethics and morals in the child.

By the end of phase three of Outer Dependence, the child is prepared to expand into the next phase of Interdependence.

This phase will take the individual to full maturity – physically, mentally, intellectually – and towards awakening and higher consciousness.

Phase Four: The World of Interdependence

The phase of Interdependence is the main creational nursery of the self. It is the melting-pot in which the ultimate and highest potential in the human may evolve. It is also like the operation and refining of a gold-mine, in which the dross is separated from the gold, which then emerges in its purified state.

We see this phase of Interdependence echoed in the macrocosm when the cosmic intergalactic network attains its full splendour of interrelatedness and stabilisation.

The growth and development of phase four generally spans the age of approximately seven to around forty and beyond. Generally, full physical maturity is attained around the age of twenty-three when all faculties and systems of the body have reached their optimum condition. Then comes the age of the intellect, mental maturity and the development of the cognitive capacity (including all the inner faculties as described earlier). The age of higher maturity, inner unfolding and spiritual awakening is frequently referred to as the age of prophethood, and takes place around the age of approximately forty years.

During Interdependence, we witness the development of the rational self, with wisdom (knowledge confirmed by subjective experience and applied) as its highest virtue. Whereas the one who has not yet attained stable maturity reacts emotionally to his hunger, fear and discomfort, the rational being knows that there are more effective ways and possibilities to achieve desired results. The rational being is able to call upon the results of previous experiences in order to ascertain an appropriate course of action (the initiative in his hand), rather than remaining the passive victim of simple reaction (as, for example, the child does).

Also, as we mature we attain maximum coordination, integration and connections. Contacts, information and names in our address books are at their fullest. Our family and relations, circle of friends, personal and social transactions and knowledge of places and systems are all at a maximum. Our network is at its optimum both in quality and quantity. We interrelate and absorb outward facts, information, and knowledge into our existing network of previous knowledge and experience. The forces of dynamic interdependence are at their fullest.

The objective of life's journey and this earthly melting-pot is for the body to serve the self as a vehicle for it to attain its ultimate goal of growth and awakening to its fullest awareness of reality. Material or worldly achievements by themselves alone can never bring us to complete and steady contentment. Finally, we need to know the origin and destiny of our life, its purpose and the nature of death.

In the next section, we introduce several models, paradigms and grids which help us to understand the real nature of human existence. When we relate or overlay these grids, or blueprints, upon the subject we are considering (human existence), they reveal, clarify and highlight certain dimensions and patterns which were hidden or obscure before. When the grids of the macrocosm and the microcosm are overlaid one upon the other, certain corresponding patterns in the two emerge.

These grids are like yardsticks, lenses or prisms. Sometimes they act like telescopes to focus outwardly, and at other times like microscopes, to focus inwardly. The objective is to focus on different dimensions and from different angles, to gain a better overall understanding of the realities in question.

The Holographic Paradigm

A hologram is a special type of optical storage system, in which each of its individual parts contains the whole image. If a holographic picture is torn in half, each of the halves will contain the entire image. If we again tear each piece in half, each quarter will still contain the entire picture. This can be continued ad infinitum until we are left with the tiniest piece of holographic photo – and it will still contain the entire image. In other words, each individual fragment or piece of hologram, no matter how small, contains the whole picture.

A key point here is that each part reflects the whole and exhibits the quality of the whole. Here we have a model where the part is from the whole, and the whole is seen in each part. The microself too has come about from the One Unique Self and reflects its attributes!

Before creation manifest, there was unseen reality. From that unific source emanated a movement towards multiple diversity. The patent to reproduce holograms that are capable of reflecting that one unific source is the true birthright of the human being.

If the human being (the human hologram) follows his innate developmental process of physical growth, cognitive and inner development, he will end up reflecting faithfully his original blueprint – a being evolved in time, but whose essence is from beyond time and is timeless. Thus if the self is like a hologram, then it might at some level reflect a holistic realm that transcends spatial and temporal boundaries. This domain is essentially the same domain of transcendental unity-in-diversity which is described and experienced by prophets, mystics and sages.

Research in physics has further led to the conclusion that physical entities which seem to be separate and discrete in space and time are actually linked or unified in an implicit, immeasurable fashion. In other words, the actual physical universe itself seems to act as a gigantic hologram, with each part expressed in the whole and the whole expressed in each part.

The human being in some ways seems like a hologram inhabiting a holographic universe. In the outer realm of space and time, things and events are indeed separated by intervals and are distinct. But beneath the surface, in the inner realm, all things and events are spacelessly, timelessly, intrinsically unified and undivided. Thus the experience of unity, oneness and other spiritual or mystical states can in a way be explained using the language of the holographic paradigm.

The Chart of Opposites: Grid of Eight

As soon as one begins to analyse, discriminate and differentiate, one realises that everything in creation is based on opposites. All physical creation or experience falls into, or may be classified by, combinations of the following:

Outer   – Inner
Sensory   – Meaning
Terrestrial – Celestial

To illustrate this, let us imagine that I am standing before you presenting this discourse. It is an outer event. You are looking at me. It is a sensory experience. We are in the material, physical world. It is therefore terrestrial. So we have an outer, sensory, terrestrial experience. Yet the purpose of my standing before you is to share with you inner knowledge. So the purpose and sharing is an inner, meaning, celestial experience. The two opposites are balanced. The root of every situation or event lies in its opposite.

Ordinary physical or material actions can be given a higher purpose and direction by awareness of the related inner event. For example, eating a meal is an outer, sensory, terrestrial event. However, if we eat with the intention to nourish our body in order that it may be used effectively by the soul, and thus carry us in good stead on the journey to greater perception and enlightenment, we see the hidden bases of the act are inner, meaning, and celestial – like a tree with balancing roots.

Another example is the uplifting of the sexual act to a higher value if one's intentions and attitude are lifted from the usual animal passions. At the physical level this act brings about a momentary state of (physical) freedom, and contentment (or peace of mind) is experienced. Nature uses this experience of desirability and temporary tranquillity to ensure the species' continuation. When one's understanding of the nature of the sexual act becomes clear, then the mystery of all other psychological complexities concerning it begins to disappear.

Generally, as the self develops and evolves, there is a trend or movement from the outer towards the inner, from the sensory towards the meaning, from the terrestrial towards the celestial. A balanced and stable situation comes about when the opposites counteract each other. Take, for example, motherly love, where its origin is traceable to inner (instinctive), meaning (connectedness) and terrestrial (material and physical). This love is expressed, however, in three ways: the outer (tenderness and embrace), the sensory (visible expressions of love), and the celestial (inexplicable beyond the world).

The one who seeks a state of health and equilibrium places himself in the middle of the spectrum of opposites. One's experiences of the outer, sensory, terrestrial will be balanced by the inner, meaning, and celestial. If any one of these aspects is not met with its opposite in any given act or situation, one experiences imbalance.

In our present society, the tendency is overwhelmingly towards the outer, sensory, and terrestrial, namely the materialistic and the physical. As a result, we witness considerable increase in social diseases, such as alcohol, drugs, illicit sex, and so on, through which we abortively attempt to seek inner, meaning, celestial experiences.

We see, for example, how untiring is the sincerely motivated social worker or therapist of the handicapped. They are dealing with physical limitations which are generally outer, sensory, and terrestrial, but their motivation is to liberate the person from his ills and handicaps. Whilst most of the actual work is at a very mundane level, the objective and motivation is of a higher dimension, giving inner meaning to their work.

Looking at the secret and undefinable attraction of a masterwork such as the ceiling of the Sistine Chapel, we see that the painting of the fresco itself is outer, sensory, and terrestrial, but the motivation and inspiration behind it were the exact opposite – inner, meaning, and celestial.

The Islamic act of worship is another perfect example of such a balance. The prescribed obligatory performance of the prayer has an outer, sensory, terrestrial formula. Yet the condition or inner state of the performer of the prayer is expected to be inner, meaning, and celestial.

All events and experiences, then, can be classified according to any of eight combinations of opposites.[2] They are:

			Example
1. Outer	– Sensory	– Terrestrial	building one's house
2. Outer	– Sensory	– Celestial	building a place of worship
3. Outer	– Meaning	– Terrestrial	seeing someone in pain
4. Outer	– Meaning	– Celestial	looking at someone praying
5. Inner	– Sensory	– Terrestrial	remembering a loved one
6. Inner	– Sensory	– Celestial	reflecting upon the stars
7. Inner	– Meaning	– Terrestrial	heart overflowing with love for all creation
8. Inner	– Meaning	– Celestial	meditating upon God

Varieties of Love

Relationships of love and friendship are classified by al-Miskawayh[3] according to the speed with which they develop and end. All of these types can be seen in ordinary day-to-day relationships.

Quick/Quick is the type of love which occurs swiftly and also dissolves quickly. The origin or drive behind this type of love is pleasure, for pleasure is quickly aroused and quickly consumed.

Quick/Slow is the second type of love, which comes about quickly, but ends or will be forgotten slowly. The root cause of this type of love is often natural goodness. For example, we love to reach those who are in need, and charitable emotions come upon us all of a sudden. We love the act of giving – generously. This goodness occurs quickly and departs from us slowly. Another example is when people of wisdom or spiritual inclination meet one another. Usually a spark of love is ignited in the heart which will last and endure for a long time.

Slow/Quick is the third type of love, and is one which occurs often in the commercial world. It occurs slowly but dissolves quickly. A business relationship builds over time and is based on mutual benefit or trust. Once that benefit is exhausted or the trust broken, then the relationship is quickly terminated. Any love that is based on benefit or existential usefulness arises and builds up slowly, but can dissolve quickly.

Slow/Slow is the love or relationship based on mature and considered goodness. It develops slowly and leaves slowly. This is usually the type of love that occurs between people based on natural harmony and compatibility between them. Whilst this type of love grows, there are often doubts, suspicion and reconfirmation, until love sets in deeply. This type of love is compounded by good will, deep faithfulness and loyalty.

In general, a relationship that builds and dissolves slowly tends to be in the domain of the higher and subtler qualities of human beings. These are the types of relationships that the mature self seeks to establish and will value in life.

Male/Female Relationships

Like everything else in this creation which is based on opposites, so also is the human male/female relationship. There is, as we experience and observe, a basic complementarity in the twin natures of man and woman that can bring about, when the two opposites meet, the right balance and equilibrium for growth and development.

As with everything else in life, at first the gross prevails over the subtle, the outer prevails over the inner and, therefore, if there is physical, material and emotional harmony, then the stage is set for the growth of the inner dimensions and spiritual awakening. First, the basic human needs must be removed in order that the energy may be directed towards fulfilling the higher needs, and here man and woman can uplift and help each other's progress.

The basic purpose of the relationship between man and woman is to assist into bringing about contentment, understanding and awakening of the inner and higher potential. We find, however, that there are differences in outlook and orientation between the two sexes. Woman's role, generally speaking, tends to be more home-related, and she naturally prefers stable and contained situations and dislikes existential uncertainties and turmoil. The male, on the other hand, tends to be more adventurous as a general rule, and to varying degrees thrives on exposure to uncertainties. He is much more the instrument of creativity and destruction: the hunter and warrior are more part of his nature.

One of woman's great influences is the stabilisation of that which is around her (by her tender and motherly nature). She is, we say, mother earth. She is the one who maintains and nourishes. She is also like water – giving earth its renewal, and will only settle upon a rock bed, not soft earth – thus the need for strong men!

A woman is at her best, generally speaking, when she has a strong and reliable man behind her. Man, conversely, is at his best when he contains a gentle and loyal woman. A woman wishes to be held in a man's embrace, to be contained, protected, desired, depended upon, and so to be content. This is why a woman often continues to mother her child long after it has grown to maturity, because that is her natural tendency, her primal purpose and role in life. Earth is the life giver, so woman too is the giver, and if she is not asked or needed to give, she will become as barren as a desert.

In the Islamic tradition, man is held a degree above woman. This additional responsibility of the male is because he is, generally speaking, biologically and emotionally steadier and hence more predictable than woman and, therefore, is given slightly greater authority over woman to care for and protect her. The male also has greater responsibility toward the female and her offspring.

In the matter of inheritance, for example, although the male receives twice that of a female, he actually usually ends up with less because he is responsible for his wife's and children's upkeep, whereas the woman is not obliged to share her inheritance with anyone else.

Marriage is worthwhile if it uplifts the husband and wife and helps in developing each towards his or her higher spiritual potential. If their relationship is conducive to this growth and development, then it can indeed be a beautiful affair. Otherwise, it will bring disappointment, unfulfilled expectations and misery. The most fortunate among us are those whose passion and devotion for our loved one has expanded to the point where we can direct that force towards the love of all creation and, ultimately, the all-encompassing Creator. It is only then that the purpose of life can be attained.

Towards Phase Five of Inner Reliance

As we emerge from the experiences of Interdependence, we begin to rely more and more on the store of experiences and inner awareness. Attaining the age of maturity, physically, emotionally and intellectually, we slowly move away from the appetites and distractions of this existence. The creational melting-pot of the world of Interdependence has served its purpose, as a laboratory in which we have tested and have been tested in situations of interaction and interrelationships. All of these have aided in spurring on and refining the development of the rational self.

At this point, we are beginning to approach the state of Inner Reliance. We begin to taste the delights of inner awakening and increase in our knowledge of the unific state. In the continuing journey, our heart becomes a reflector of the truth. We gain better discrimination of the world and our relationship to it. As a result, our inner practices of self-development increase, reflected in virtuous outer behaviour. At this stage, we are able to see more clearly the stages of the journey through which we have evolved.

The Earth and the World

There is an important distinction to be made here between the earth (*ard*) and the world (*dunya*). The earth is the natural, creational world, whereas the world represents man's attachments and desires to it. Earth is neutral and passive, and is simply the planet itself. It is the necessary physical melting-pot, the arena in which creation, development and evolution take place, where worldly attachments and suffering are experienced, and where the love and quest for the Garden and peace are practised. From the earth emanates life, and to it return the bodies of the dead. It is an objective, healthy and rational phenomenon. Within it, much irrationality and confusion can take place. The earth is tolerant of the world it brings about. It is most patient and generous, for it only reflects the nature of the Creator.

The Arabic word for the world is *dunya*, from the root *dana*, which means to be accessible or low (in the sense of abased). It refers to the attachment, instant pleasure and desirability that sets in when a person is interacting with the events that take place on earth.

Dunya is the world as we make it. Each of us has his personal world, whereas the earth itself is always the same in essence. All of us are on the same earth, but each one of us is engrossed to varying degrees in his own world.

In Islamic tradition, the world is always regarded as that which causes one to be distracted from the true purpose of creation. It is related in the Qur'an:

> And what else is the life of this world but a sport and a pastime? (6:32)

A Prophetic tradition states that this world is a prison for the believer, and a garden for the one who denies the truth. Another tradition relates that he who loves this world causes harm to himself in the next life, and he who loves the next life will neglect this world, that is, he will be neither attached to nor dependent upon this world.

We naturally prefer desirable experiences which last forever to those which are transitory and short-lived. It is related in a Prophetic tradition that love of this world is at the head of every wrong action or wrongdoing. The Prophet Muhammad further says, 'What is there for me in this world? I am like the traveller who stops to rest for awhile under the shade of a tree, before moving on.'

One of our traditions relates the following narrative concerning the Prophet Jesus. The world was revealed to him in the image of an old crone who had adorned herself, and he asked her how many times she had been married. She replied that she could not count them all. He asked if her husbands had died or divorced her. She replied that she had killed all of them. He then said, 'Woe to your striving husbands, who did not heed the lesson of those who passed away before them.'

Ali ibn Abi Talib[4] comments in his description of the world, 'How shall I describe an abode whose beginning is difficulty and whose end is destruction? Whatever of it is allowed, you are accountable for, and whatever is forbidden, you will be punished for. He who rises above it will be afflicted and he who is in need of it will be saddened. He who strives towards it, will lose it, and he who turns away from it will see it coming towards him. He who sees through it will have insight, and he who looks at it with fascination will be blinded.'

One sage has said, 'This world is the mother of death, and whoever settles in it will not be content with it. No matter what your position in it, you will be discontent.' This is proof that it is a transient stage and that one can never be content with it.

Socrates said that the treachery of the world comes very quickly to whoever trusts it, and yet comes little to those who do not trust it. He who loves this world will sorrow greatly and his enemies will be many. But for him who is an ascetic in the world, his heart will be at rest, and those who are jealous of him will be few.

A story is related about the woman saint, Rabi'ah,[5] that there was a gathering at her place where many men of wisdom and gnosis were present, and they were speaking against the world and its vices. She kept her silence until they all had their say, then she said, 'He who loves a thing mentions it often, either by praising it or by denouncing it. So if this world were not in your hearts, why do you mention it so often?'

A tradition relates that the Prophet Jesus said that one who builds a home for himself on the waves of the ocean – and that is this world – should not expect it to be an abode of lasting reliability and certainty.

Our teachings do not imply renunciation of this world, nor is the world ever to be considered an illusion. Its very transiency impels us to see beyond it in order to free ourselves from its snares and attachments.

We have seen that this world and all its pleasures are passing affairs that have no permanent reality in themselves. By investigating and interacting with the world, the self develops the faculties of reasoning, discrimination and intellect. So the world and one's relationship with it as we have mentioned earlier is a training-ground for evolvement towards the higher self.

The sad truth is that he who falls in love with this world will be forever in sorrow and in ever-increasing pain. It is like one who is in love with something that is ultimately an illusion. How can there be any fruit from such a transient and everchanging relationship? It is like a person who watches the waves on the surface and completely forgets the deep ocean below them: all his thoughts and vision are turned to the waves which are only localised surface events. He misses the vision of the vast world of the ocean depths by staring at its changing surface only.

The people of reality, on the other hand, are those who are absorbed in witnessing the greatness and limitlessness of the ocean. This absorbs them to such an extent that they are hardly concerned with the waves, except as a certain aspect of the total reality. They know how shallow is the wave compared with the ocean's vastness and depth. They also know that the wave derives its power and energy from the ocean, and that it is only a changing ripple on the surface of a vast and fathomless sea. Such is the transient nature of this world, according to the people of wisdom and reality.

As we gain greater discrimination of the world and begin to taste the delights of the vast unific state, our inner practices of self-development increase, resulting in more fruitful and positive behaviour. We now turn to a few of the practices and teachings of self-development.

Doing Without (*zuhd*)

Zuhd is normally translated as asceticism, but its real meaning is doing without. It means turning away from something desirable by turning to something else that is more desirable. So he who exchanges attachment and desire for this world with love and yearning for the next world is an ascetic in that he prefers the next life to this. Another definition of *zuhd* is to take little in order to give back more.

Turning away in itself as an experience has many degrees. There are those who turn away from this world, yet their attachment and love for it lingers. They appear to be ascetic, but their hearts have not been disconnected. This sort of doing without brings about degradation of the self because it is hardship without the sweetness, freedom and bliss that comes by truly turning away.

Doing without does not mean renunciation of the world. We cannot reject this world for we are in it; we can reject only our attachment to it. We live in this world while at the same time we must recognise that we are not of it, like a rider who stops briefly to rest in the shade before travelling on.

It is for this reason that prophets, sages and gnostics see themselves as strangers in this world, and thus they take neither solace nor contentment in it. Their real love and contentment lie elsewhere, in a permanent abode which they tap within their own hearts.

Ali ibn Abi Talib said that asceticism does not mean that you do not own anything, but that nothing owns you.

Reflection and Retreat

Sometimes one leaves the company of others for awhile and enters a retreat, because of the trouble and affliction that come from people and the world. At other times, leaving people can bring about increased love and intimacy with Reality. In either case, the practice of retreat is to be used as a temporary exercise when a state of reflection, devotion or inner spiritual growth is desired. Retreat as an outer practice is never recommended as a permanent measure.

It is related by one of the masters that he who chooses retreat in preference to companionship must be empty of all other remembrances and wants. Otherwise, he will be tyrannised in his retreat by the desires and mental agitations which follow him.

It is also said that one must think deeply as to whom one is with in retreat. If one's intimacy in retreat is with the Creator, then it will be the same whether one is in the vast deserts, the high caves, or the marketplace in the company of men. We see by this that the goal of retreat is to be in a state of inner alertness and awakening in the cave of one's heart at all times and in all places.

By entering a retreat, there are many benefits that help to release the dormant springs of knowledge within, for this cannot occur unless the heart is empty and one's distractions are left behind.

Right Companionship

Just as one's character and intellect improve by being with noble and virtuous beings, equally, companionship with people who are corrupt and evil will bring about one's corruption. A Prophetic tradition relates that he who sits with a person of virtue is like a man who sits with someone wearing musk: if one does not benefit from exchanges with him, at least his fragrance will bring one goodness. But he who sits with a person of vice is like he who sits next to the blacksmith. If one is not burnt by the sparks of his furnace, then his smoke will suffocate one.

Another tradition relates that there are three types of companions. One is like food that one cannot do without; the second is like medicine – one needs it from time to time; and the third is like sickness – one can well do without it. This latter type one should avoid keeping company with.

In keeping company, it is important to have compatibility of character and a relationship that will bring about harmony and goodness for both parties. For the one who is sensitive and looks for inner meanings cannot be a close companion of one who is gross and vulgar, and one who is mindful and reflective cannot be with one who is shallow and foolish. One who is open-hearted and loves creation cannot be with another who is hateful and full of doubt. Worst of all, one who believes in the next life, and regards this life as a preparation for it, cannot be happy with one who regards this life as the only experience and denies all else.

So it is important for us to consider, test and select our companions before we befriend them. It is akin to testing the soil before we place a seed in it. In this vein it is very important that we consider carefully the compatibility of people before marriage so that we give the experience the best chance for a healthy and desirable outcome.

When a person finds a companion in this world, it is very important to cherish him or her and to be loyal. It is not a common occurrence to find one who is a true brother, or sister. Indeed, it is a rare commodity, and like all rare commodities, it has to be guarded and cherished. It is very important for us to develop the art of confirming and conserving our friends and companions, for if we do not, it is like one who spends his time collecting wealth, and once he has acquired it, cannot keep it or look after it. Therefore the effort to preserve and care for those who are real friends is very important and should not be neglected.

Relationship with Others

A Prophetic tradition enjoins us to reach out to those who have cut off relationships with us and to give to those who have wronged us. It also states that all creation is the family of God, and those whom God loves most are those who are most useful and helpful to creation. Another Prophetic tradition relates that serving one's brother for an hour is better than remaining in devotional solitude for a year.

It is also important to consider the obligations upon us regarding our friends, and to constantly nurture and nourish that relationship. We must remember that people will change and go through different states and stages until a time when they mature and are developed fully. When that happens, the relationship becomes one of perfection because the people of purity and love have a bond that is borne of subtle or sublime factors that are beyond themselves. They have reached a stage of recognising the one self, the universal self, and yet manifesting in different bodies. From the one self we outwardly experience separate entities. When the hearts are clear and the self is purified, we experience steady, tranquil, deep and reliable relationships.

Models of Wayfaring

In Islam, many illustrations, analogies and models are given to show the different stages of self-evolvement. The analogy of the traveller or the journey is frequently used to describe the seeker's ascent from a state of ignorant darkness to illumination and awareness.

The models below are three such examples. The stages within a given model naturally overlap, and the entire spectrum within the model remains active to varying degrees of intensity within the human self throughout one's life.

In the first model, for example, the saint is not wholly exempt from recognising a glimpse of the commanding self within him.

The Seven Stations of the Self

1. *The commanding self.* The first and lowest station is that of the commanding self (*al-nafs al-ammara*). This is the station of one who is not sufficiently developed inwardly, who is crude and childish, base, egoistic and selfish, with little concern or connection with other than self-gratification.

This is the self that is dominated by the physical body, and follows mainly the gratification of sensual pleasure and fleeting desires. This state draws the heart towards its lower and negative extreme. This facet of the self is the abode of most vices and the source of all bad characters.

The characteristics of the commanding self encompass meanness, greed, envy, jealousy, ignorance, self-importance, pride, glory, presumption, arrogance, sensuality, anger, violence, insensitivity, lack of insight, and vile manners, interference in what does not concern one, making fun and mocking others, avarice, hatred, qualities of rigidity and dogma, opacity, and the inability to be reached or to form stable relationships. The colour related to the commanding self is blue. It is the blue of intense heat in the middle of the flame.

2. *The reproachful self.* The second station is the reproachful self (*al-nafs al-lawwama*). In this station, the self develops some sense of right and wrong. It begins to have glimpses of insight into its own conduct and occasionally even blames itself for wrong behaviour. The reproachful self does have some measure of awareness and discrimination, but that reproach usually occurs after the event. It is like a crack, so to speak, in the solid frame of the commanding self, that gives rise to the reproachful self with a slight degree of flexibility and awareness.

Its characteristics are acting upon whims of the moment,

conceit, having to do with self-image, vanity, injustice, bias, backbiting, slander, lying, and excessive love of leadership. Its colour is yellow. This colour is located on the edge of the flame and it represents descending and decaying energy.

3. *The inspired self.* The third station is the inspired self (*al-nafs al-mulhama*). This condition of the self is supple and dynamic, and therefore leads to vulnerability. It is an inter-space between good and bad. The keeping of good company and right guidance is necessary at this stage for the self to evolve. This is also the station of love, and of being in love. We generally find this type of self attractive because it reminds us of a free spirit, as it is less attached and more willing to change course, and is freer of inhibitions and attachments.

The inspired self is considered easy to treat, for it is not tethered. It has no firm anchorage or rigid boundaries. It is inspired and mobile like quicksilver. One may think of it as mercury – flexible and mobile, but elusive and difficult to steady and grasp. This type of self may begin to be developed and groomed once it has been contained, stabilised and nurtured within a stable base. In this state is the danger of excessive love and wonderment of nature, even worship. This state can be found in scientists, painters, musicians and artists, because of the preponderance of wonderment and marvels that are experienced in their arenas.

The characteristics of the inspired self are generosity, forgiveness, tolerance, endurance, good opinion, acknowl-edging faults, an open-faced smiling countenance, love of peace and meditation, contentment with the decree, and having the ability to weep easily, which is the opposite of the commanding self. Its colour is red, which is lively and vivid and at the centre of a flame.

4. *The certain self.* The fourth station is the certain self (*al-nafs al-mutma'ina*). Here, the self attains confidence and security by knowledge and experience. The self can journey back to its origins, to recall and become inwardly awakened to the reality that everything, including itself, is from reality and to that reality is its return, by the grace and mercy of the same reality.

It is that self whose light has been ignited by the spark of the heart, and has overcome the lower characteristics and taken on the higher qualities. It is content, not out of ignorance, but with knowledge. Its contentment is a result of the knowledge that it has done its best within its limits, and therefore all is well. The heart is clear and it is tranquil, content, and steady with faith and trust.

Amongst the characteristics of the certain self are unsolicited generosity, dependence on the Creator, freedom from fear of need or attachment, spontaneous awareness of the rule of the opposites in the world, sincerity, contentment, freedom in action, contentment with the decree, absence of agitation, gratitude for the perfection of creation and one's place in it, fear and dread of trespassing the bounds (for fear at the beginning of the path is knowledge, fear in the middle is ignorance, and fear at the end is delight), being on a clear path, acting only out of certainty, a heart full of trust, faith, certainty, knowledge, right action and security. Its colour is white, reflecting all the colours (and holding or absorbing none).

5. *The contented self*. The fifth station is the contented self (*al-nafs al-radhiya*). It is the station of the one who sees the truth always, in every situation and in everything.

Its characteristics are sincerity, innocent genuineness, continuing caution and fear of trespassing the bounds, scrupulousness, total inner courtesy, and avoiding any desire except that of knowledge and the pleasure of reality. The contented self is childlike in its simplicity. It is spontaneous, always living in the moment. Its colour is green, the colour of growth and life on earth – the pleasant and 'middle' colour.

6. *The self that everything is contented with*. The sixth station is the self that pleases and satisfies the rest of creation (*al-nafs al-mardhiya*). If one is knowingly content with one's Creator, then everything in creation is content and in harmony with oneself. This is the station where the world of the macrocosm is in equilibrium with the microcosm.

This self overflows with mercy and love towards all creation, is devoted to the service of others, and is in complete balance in that interspace between the outer world and the inner reality. This self's responsibilities in the outer world do not veil it from the joy and bliss of inner realities, nor do the inner delights blind it from outer obligations. Here, the self does not know anger, greed, revenge or hatred. Its colour is black, which absorbs all the other colours. All shades and colours stop here.

7. *The perfected self.* The ultimate station is the perfected self (*al-nafs al-kamila*), or the station of pure beingness.

Of this station, the Prophet Muhammad said, 'He who knows himself, knows his Lord.' He is the one who knows himself to be an interspace, combined of a physical vehicle (or body), and a spirit of divine origin that rides upon the vehicle as a means of witnessing and arriving back to its blissful abode – the eternal Garden. It also means that he is where the beautiful names of God (the divine attributes of Reality) are gathered and known.

The perfected self is in the state of unific knowledge, oneness in divine unity, the state of pure consciousness and pure beingness.

Levels of Certainty

Another model of the stages of inner awakening and awareness can be described as the unfolding of three levels of certainty.

The first level is the knowledge of certainty (*'ilm al-yaqin*). This is the level of mental and intellectual understanding or appreciation of an experience: for example, we hear a report that there is a fire in the forest. As we have past experiences of both fire and forest, we develop a mental image of the forest on fire and reach a certain image or understanding of the event.

The second level is that of clear or witnessing certainty (*'ayn al-yaqin*). This is when one actually sees a fire in the forest – a direct witnessing of the source, or origin, of the event.

The third level is the truth of certainty (*haqq al-yaqin*). This is when one actually undergoes an interactive experience – when one actually gets burnt in the forest fire. Here final and absolute truth of the event takes place and unquestionably imparts its reality – the burning sensation and total experience.

There is, however a final stage beyond the three described and that is the truth of truth (*haqq al-haqq*). Here one can no longer refer to a duality of experiencer and experienced. It means one is completely consumed by the fire, engulfed by it, and completely transformed by it. This is a realm beyond existential or describable experience. It belongs to another level of consciousness and another dimension.

The Four Unveilings

Another model of the journey of the self is given by the great Sufi master, Mulla Sadra.[6] He uses the analogy of the wayfarer to describe man's journey from the state of ignorant darkness to one of illuminated awareness. In this model he describes four stages of unveilings along the journey. It begins when man reaches a point where he realises there is no lasting fulfilment in the existential, changing world.

We all experience at different times in our life the desire for tranquillity and seclusion. When worldly difficulties and failures mount, we may wish to leave it all. Many of us go through a period when the monastic life seems an appropriate refuge and it is during these times that we want to turn our backs on creation. It is often at times of the greatest difficulty and confusion that we turn towards the path of discovery of the source in order to understand the position we have landed in. It is when the actors in the play begin to question the plot that we seek to know the author and ask for an explanation.

When we reach this point and realise that there can be no lasting fulfilment in the existential, changing world, we take flight to the edge of the known, which is the unknown dimension. Here the first stage of unveiling begins.

The four stages which follow illustrate the main stations that the successful wayfarer attains in his journey. Throughout his life, he will continue to experience the entire spectrum of states to varying degrees of intensity. What Mulla Sadra wishes to emphasise here is the established station that the wayfarer attains, rather than simply the passing, temporary states which he will continue to experience from time to time in this life.

The First Unveiling: From Creation to the Creator

The first barrier to cross, or the first unveiling, is from the creation to the Creator. The wayfarer flees from the confusing, physical and material universe of opposites to another dimension – the dependable, real and reassuring world of the unified field of reality. The silence within is the knock on the inner door.

The unveiling of the first barrier involves tearing away veils both of darkness and light that exist between the seeker and the spiritual reality within. Then the ascent can begin from the station of the lower self to the station of the intellect, and from the station of the intellect to the station of the spirit, and from the station of the spirit to the farthest goal of supreme splendour. If the wayfarer succeeds in reaching the goal, the final veils are lifted and he is annihilated by the death of the transitory, dissolved and submerged in the divine source.

The Second Unveiling: With the Creator by the Courtesy of the Creator

The second unveiling is the journey across the barrier to knowledge of the Creator. The wayfarer is now exposed to Reality by the courtesy of Reality. He moves totally in the inner realm. He attains gnosis. His essence, attributes and actions become annihilated in the divine essence. In this journey, he sees through His seeing, hears through His hearing and knows through His knowing.

When the inner journey and discoveries are taking place, the wayfarer looks for greater confirmation of these openings. He is like someone who discovers that he is truly a guest, and that his Host is most generous and understanding. The wayfarer then hopes for this condition to last and for him to remain in this refuge. As though he sees his image in a mirror for the first time, he seeks confirmation and establishment of what he has seen.

The Third Unveiling: From the Creator to Creation by the Permission of the Creator

The completion of the second unveiling marks the start of the third journey. In this, the wayfarer returns from the Creator back to creation by the permission of the Creator. In this journey, he is armed with the knowledge of truth.

The wayfarer's state of self-annihilation is complete and he now attains full sobriety and balance. He subsists through the subsistence of the Creator. He returns to creation by the authority of the Creator with the knowledge of the unveiling.

The nature of life does not change and it carries on with its ups and downs. There is no avoidance by anyone of experiencing these outer waves which occur at the surface above the still depths of the ocean. So when the wayfarer is established in his station, he returns to creation with all its turmoil. However, the wayfarer, because of his knowledge of the nature of the ocean, is now far more able to deal with its changing surface. The waves are of little significance and the storms are relative puffs of wind compared to the stable mass of the deep.

The Fourth Unveiling: With Creation by the Authority of the Creator

The wayfarer then embarks upon the fourth stage, which is to be among creation by the authority of the Creator, when nothing else remains but service in the bliss of knowledge. The seeker observes and recognises creation and humanity, their behaviour and needs. He knows the good that they bring about and the evil that they cause, and what causes them happiness and what brings them misery.

In all this, he is with the truth, for his entire being has been submerged in reality, and the service rendered by him to other beings does not distract him from inner divine bliss, steadfastness and certainty. The fully realised being is now in the ultimate unitive state. He is completely in outer service of humanity and in inner abandonment, freedom and joy.

When reality in all its various aspects is unveiled to the wayfarer and he is established in the knowledge of truth within, a new outlook towards creation emerges. The awakened being sees the divine thread through all existence and therefore is qualified to serve with selflessness, with no danger to creation or to himself. When the individual self has aligned itself with the original unified reality, the flowering of the spiritual being has occurred. It is this unveiling that is referred to as 'with creation by the authority of the Creator'. Wherever the enlightened being looks, he sees the trace and the mark of the Creator. He is now an agent of transformation, a loyal slave to the Divine Master and a freed being with no choice but to reflect what comes to his pure heart. This is the state of a prophet with his people – outwardly the same as any of them, inwardly tuned to his eternal origin.

Summary

We have seen that as the power of discrimination matures and the faculties of cognition evolve and develop, they begin to supersede and control the physical and all other material tendencies. We can say of this person that he has mastered the art of the unitive state. He has mastered the art of dynamic submission. He has integrated and connected with both his inner and outer environment. He understands the interrelationships and the interplay of events instantly, as there is no longer any dispersion or confusion at any point within him. There is no longer an observer and the observed. There is no 'two', or duality in his existential make-up, for all is seen with the unific viewpoint.

So our traveller has reached a condition where he understands new situations instantaneously. He has entered into a state of integrated ecology of the unitive life. We can say he is fully realised, awakened. He is in complete inner tranquillity yet dynamically alive and active. The outer humility and abasement of such a being is balanced by an inner joy and elevation in the true spiritual heritage.

As we enter Phase Five of Inner Reliance, the rational individual has reached a station where he has taken himself as far as possible in discipline, in keeping to the bounds, in being aware of his inner state and of what impinges upon him from the outer world. He therefore becomes a fully mature, reliable human being, who is at the stage of achieving full potential of the self.

Phase Five: The World of Inner Reliance

Entry to the stage of Inner Reliance occurs when one reaches the highest possible station in physical, mental and intellectual maturity and wisdom and has attained the virtue of justice. At this stage one is in the best state of equilibrium and balance, acquired through our experiential knowledge and stability, the overall result of true submission and surrender to reality.

With the advent of the fifth phase of Inner Reliance, the dynamic interrelationships of phase four will be superseded by increasing inner awakenings, knowledge and tranquillity. The rational self has evolved and has become established through self-knowledge. As spiritual unfoldment increases, one experiences the inner joy of discovering the prophetically revealed truths and knowledge. The origin and early evolvement of inner reliance begins early on, and continues for the rest of one's life. Whilst a person lives, there inevitably will exist a certain degree of interdependence.

One way of describing this state of Inner Reliance is to call it the point of realisation or awakening, of inner death, or the annihilation of the self. That experience is the equivalent of certainty in the station of the truth of truth discussed earlier. It is that level of certainty as when one actually experiences the fire and is consumed by it. At that point, one knows that the entity called the self, that is, the 'I' or 'me', is none other than a passing shadow and is dependent on a higher and all-pervading reality. A point is reached where mystery and fear are lifted, and one has experienced and tasted death of the self during conscious life.

Once self-knowledge is mastered, one attains a joy and happiness which cannot be measured by any of the normal senses. This joy is of a higher value, and gives greater solace and comfort, than anything else we can seek or find in this world.

It is during phase five that the final unveiling of the self takes place, which is described earlier in the model of Mulla Sadra. He describes this stage in man's journey as being with creation in truth, and this is the final journey toward complete commitment to reality. In traditional Hindu society, for example, a man, after raising a family and providing for its welfare, goes off into the woods for a period of spiritual retreat. After attaining enlightenment to whatever degree possible, he then returns to society in order to teach and to serve others. He is amongst creation with the licence of surrender and knowledge.

When the gnostic returns to society, it may appear on the surface that the degree of his interaction with others has not changed, or even increased. The actual situation is different. He has returned only to share and teach the knowledge that he has gained, and to serve selflessly. As far as the individual is concerned, all he is doing is reconfirming his inner satisfaction and reliance whilst recognising other people's stages of evolution and development, and guiding them onward. He has already passed through these stages and has reached a summit within himself, and thus can guide those who follow with patience, compassion and understanding, and with no expectations or attachments.

What appears as outer expectation or dependence is only nature's way of winning others over, so to speak. It is not contrived nor laced with miracles, for it is a natural and real way, by familial and societal interdependence for an enlightened man to guide his people. The awakened one will, from this viewpoint, reflect and realise that throughout all existence everyone has been imitating or emulating one or another of the divine attributes, or actions of the Creator. Everyone loves and emulates correctly or perversely the beautiful qualities and names of God.

The Beautiful Names of God

The divine attributes are known as the beautiful names of God and they are commonly referred to as the ninety-nine names, although in fact there is no end to the beautiful names – for God is limitless.

Each one of us at one time or another wishes to be self-sufficient, supreme or all-powerful. We sometimes emulate the all-powerful ruler, the sovereign king, the most glorious one, the greatest, the most praiseworthy, the victorious one, the exalted, the giver of life, the creator of death, the creator of all things, the precious one, the wise, the just, the generous, the compassionate, the all-forgiving, the nourisher, the provider, the forbearing, and the patient one.

We desire these attributes or virtues because we intrinsically recall their source and their meanings within us. That is why basic morals and virtues everywhere in the world are at the outset similar, because they are founded on an implanted inner reality within each of us.

The truly realised being, the one who has qualified and passed the test, is necessarily one who has entered properly into the unific state and has connected outward reality with the inner knowledge of reality. He is the one who has become that pivotal interlink. He or she is the master of outer knowledge and understanding and the possessor of inner awareness and gnosis. This is the state of the real lover of truth.

Who is the Realised Being?

The fully realised being is the one who has returned to the source of one's origin, the pure state of divine unity. It is the original, adamic state, for Adam was originally in the pure and unified state in the Garden of bliss. He was given everything and had no whims, thoughts, or desires, manifesting only inspired and divinely guided continuous submission. He was in the realm of pure consciousness, the realm of joy and contentment.

Then a voice arose, a wave on the adamic consciousness of being, a whisper that cut through the state of pure submission. A different moment came about – the realm of our own existence based on opposite forces and energies. So Adam descended from the unified field into a realm of duality, a realm based on opposites where both right and wrong could be experienced. It is of course in this realm that the faculty of discrimination develops.

Adam was placed in this worldly condition in order to evolve in discrimination by being tested, so that he could develop towards a state of perfect equilibrium and contentment based on knowledge, differentiation and on a primal experience, for he was originally conceived in the Garden of absolute bliss.

Mankind, in essence, originated by command from the realm of divine unity, and has been placed in this realm of duality so that in every situation, he must discriminate between the two thresholds of good and evil. By this he may emerge, awakened from duality, and return to his original state.

Towards the Non-time Zone

All of us in this life are like people under water, nearly drowning, but not always realising it. Occasionally, by the force of a sudden tide or undercurrent, sometimes consciously and sometimes not, we are forced upwards and our head emerges out from below the surface for a glimpse of life above water. These are occasional glimpses of a higher dimension of reality. Transcendental experiences are of this nature. Even if we fall back again, that glimpse will have left an indelible mark, and that brilliant image or vision of the world above water will never leave us. It is as if a reunion had taken place. We are not sea creatures, after all! We are not people of the world. We are simply in this world, but do not belong to it. Our origin is from another zone, timeless, in the Garden of unspeakable delight. Once we have seen true reality, we know thenceforth that we belong to that truth. No amount of treasures in the sea will ever satisfy us again. We will constantly yearn for that tantalising glimpse.

The point at which one sees nothing other than the infinite bounty and magnificence of creation is like emerging from underwater. The next level is the return to the non-time zone. It is the entry to the phase where there is no longer any possibility of action or interaction of unification between mind and heart, or of seeing opposites. It is a phase without time, which is why it is called eternity. The metamorphosis into the next phase – by gnosis – can take place before death and thereby fulfil the ultimate purpose of life, otherwise, this state will be experienced after physical death.

Our state in the next life, whether it be in the Garden of Paradise or the Fire of Hell, is the outcome of actions that have taken place during the earthly existence. One's state in the next life is only as good as the station to which the self had risen in this earthly life; the next life is a reflection or true continuation of the quality of this life.

Death is actually an interspace between this life and the next. It is the last stage in this world of creation and marks the end of the journey in this life. It is also the first stage in the next life, the next realm of consciousness, and marks the beginning of the ongoingness of the self in the next realm, which is the state of pure consciousness beyond time and biological limitations.

The Next Consciousness

We notice that every self or soul wants to live, and hates death. This wish is, in fact, an indicator that the source or origin of the self is eternal. Its purpose in life is to complete and perfect itself by itself. The fact that the soul wants to abide forever and loves continuity is itself a proof that herein lies its true nature. It originates from and belongs to another dimension and existence – that of eternity or timelessness. We know that in this existence, physical continuation of life is impossible, given that our present world contains decay and death from the moment of birth. Where would the self acquire any idea of living forever, except from an innate primal awareness of the infinite realm where death has no domain? There is nothing in nature that does not stem from a cause or reason.

Thus we see that one reason that the self hates death is its deep, subconscious awareness of its own eternal ongoingness. But there is also a wisdom behind hating one's own death, and that is in order to preserve one's body. We must ensure its continuity, care for and protect it while it serves as our vehicle on our journey to growth and higher consciousness, until we have completed our knowledge and awakening.

The Descent and Ascent of the Self according to the Qur'an

We are given several references in the Qur'an which describe the self in its descent from the realm of divine unity to this world of duality.

> And He it is Who has brought you into being from a single soul [self]. (6:99)

> Your creation or your rising is only like a single soul [self]. (31:28)

> He created you from a single being. (39:6)

> He it is Who created you from a single being [self]. (7:189)

Thus we understand that the genesis of the self, or soul, is unific in origin. Provided that the self evolves in the path of its intended destiny, it will ultimately reach the comprehension of its root and thereby complete its purposeful journey. There are some who say that if the self had its origin before the existence of our physical body, that earlier existence must have been in the presence of the absolute divine light. When does its connection with the physical body veil the self from its knowledge of its origin in divine light?

Although the self exists in the world of natural bodies and material phenomena, it exists in its pure form in the world of the intellect which is a world of pure light. In the world of the intellect, the soul is not barred or deprived from its own perfection. However, there is certain knowledge and experience that the soul could not obtain unless it descended into the world of creation, as we have already mentioned. By descending to the body, new horizons are opened to the soul that would not have been perceived in its realm of pure consciousness and light.

The descent and ascent of the soul is referred to in another verse of the Qur'an:

> We created man in the best of forms, then We brought

him down to the lowest of the low, except those who
believe [trust] and do good works. (95:4–6)

The Qur'an also speaks of the story of Adam's descent
from the Garden.

And We said, Descend from it, all of you, until such
time there comes to you from Us, the guidance. And
those who follow Our guidance, there is no fear upon
them nor will they ever grieve. (20:123)

The descent is referred to again in another verse.

Descend from it, some of you enemies of the others, and
there is for you a brief respite in this earth and provision
in it for a time. (7:24)

These references suggest that there was an original unific
state from which we have descended in order to rediscover it
in a subjective and objective fashion as we complete the full
loop of descent and ascent. There is a similar position in this
existence with respect to physical objects. For every object
has a fixed reality in the abode of God's will that preceded
existence. In that reality, these objects are saved from any
change or destruction. But here in this world, all things are
under the influence of decay, change and destruction. It
says in the Qur'an:

And God will wipe out what He wills and He will
establish what He wills, and the source of the book is
with him. (13:39)

The source of the book means the permanent decree that
is, the universal laws that will never change. This world is
subject to change, birth, growth and destruction, but the
origin of all things in this world is from another dimension
that never changes – and that is the source of the book.
Ali ibn Abi Talib said, 'The Creator has mercy upon one
who knows whence, in what, and whither', meaning, whence the self originated before its descent, in what state is the
self and how does it manifest and interact in this world, and
whither is its final destination after this life. So the Creator's

mercy is experienced by those who know where they have come from, the state they are in now, and whither they are going. This knowledge is the foundation of ultimate security, certainty, lasting happiness and contentment. He also said, 'Let him prepare his intellect and let him be from among the sons of the next life, for he has come from the next life and to it he will return.'

Concerning the essence of the self, Ali ibn Abi Talib also said, 'Know that the human consciousness is the greatest evidence of God upon His creation, and it is the book that He wrote with His hand. The human consciousness contains the collection of the images of all the worlds and it is the abbreviation of the permanent Tablet,[7] and it is the straight way to every good action. It is the bridge between this world and the next, and the way that connects between the Garden and the Fire.'

Those who have discovered the truth about the descent and ascent of the soul agree that the descent of the soul to this world does not in any way permanently harm it. On the contrary, the soul retains all its possibilities and potentialities, and the reason it has come is to benefit from this world. The soul will benefit from this world by knowing and understanding the nature of the material, physical reality. It will come to know the world's true outer and inner nature, the good and bad things that emanate from it, and the duality that it is built upon.

By descent to this world of nature and the fact that the self has given the body its sentiency and its power and life, it has come to know what the angels are deprived of. The self comes to know all these creational realities in their totality. The feeding of the body and its nourishment is only a pale reflection of the feeding and the nourishment of the soul through knowledge acquired by itself.

There is in the body of original Islamic traditions an enormous variety of parables and examples referring to the descent of the soul and the capturing of the soul in the body, where it is imprisoned, like a caged bird. These teachings demonstrate that the soul has a reality and an existence prior to that of the body, and that its existence was in a world or dimension beyond our human comprehension. The soul, or self, will return to that existence just as it has come from it.

One must not reproach the self or look down upon it if it leaves the abode of the intellect and dwells in the physical world, because it is capable of encompassing both worlds. The self is of this nature because it is both the last of the noble divine essences and the first of the natural sensed essences. When it enters the world that can be sensed, it does not lose its inherent nobility; on the contrary, it infuses that world with its powers and will adorn it and add to its glory.

The Return of the Soul

Physical death is the beginning of the journey of the soul back to its origins, in the same way that the beginning of this natural life is the end of the descent of the soul from its source. Natural life is the product of that descent, and death is the beginning of the return of the self, as we have described earlier.

The Agony and the Reward of the Grave

Upon death, one will experience oneself as one had left this world. But already in one's imagination at the point of death, one sees oneself in the grave and senses the agonies one may suffer there as a result of one's earthly actions and transgressions. If one's earthly actions were good, one will imagine pictures of the Garden that is to come. This is called the reward of the grave. These two descriptions echo the tradition that says the grave is either the meadow of the Garden or the pit of the Fire.

The Interspace between this World and the Next

The time spent in the grave awaiting the final Day of Reckoning[8] is an intermediate stage between the world of matter and physicality, and the next creation. The parallel of this intermediate stage is like that of the development of the foetus in the womb. The self, or soul, continues to await the moment when it will be reborn on the Day of Reckoning. That is why we say, if a person dies, his 'small' Day of Reckoning has occurred, because he will be reborn in the interspace, which is the womb of the earth. The universal

Day of Reckoning will be an event in which all of creation will partake at the same time.

The Nature of the Soul in the Next Consciousness

Souls in this life hang on to their bodies, and that is how they manifest, whereas, in the next life, or next consciousness, one's manifestation and state will be according to one's degree of awakening and evolvement. One's inner reality will be reflected in how one appears in the next life. One will be restyled in a manner appropriate to one's degree of inner awakening. We realise, then, that one's manifestation in the Garden of the next life is nothing other than in the image that was sustained by the self according to what it had wished for, desired and earned in this life.

The experience of the Garden, or the next consciousness – that is, its fruits, streams and mansions – are brought about by the self according to its deeds, actions and orientation in this life before death. We ourselves bring about our own experience of the Garden or Hell – or whatever is in between – whether in this life or the next.

Also, the nature of the Fire is none other than the nature of this world and its base, ever-changing worldliness. The abode of the Fire, its afflictions and suffering, is neither separate from nor independent of this present world. Rather, it is an additional creation, an additional development. Its origins and beginnings are essentially of this world, but have been transposed into the next realm of consciousness. It is, however, a part of this total creational reality.

The Garden is a picture of God's mercy, and it is related to His essence. In the same way, the Fire is a picture of the anger or displeasure of God. But anger is not of His essence, it is part of the creational reality. Thus we can say that the Garden exists by its own essence, but the Fire has an existence only because people follow its way.

The Day of Reckoning

As far as the Day of Reckoning, or Resurrection, is concerned, it is the life into which the soul finally emerges from the dust of the images of the grave, in just the same way that the newborn emerges from the womb. The difference between being in the grave and the Day of Resurrection parallels the difference between being in the womb and being born.

For as long as the soul is not reborn and has not emerged from the belly of the earth, it cannot reach the expanse of its next abode, or consciousness.

This rebirth, however, is achieved in this life by men of gnosis who have attained self-awakening through the death of the personal will. This is what is referred to as the death, or annihilation, of the self in God, and what Jesus meant when he said that one will not reach the Kingdom of Heaven until one is born again. For others who have not arrived at this experience and have not awoken, its truth will be realised at the point of natural biological death, at which time they will come to know.

The Return, or the Next Creation (Consciousness)

There are many levels of understanding and certainty about the return to the next realm of consciousness.

The simplest level of understanding holds to the belief that all of the affairs of the next life, including the agony of the grave, the Day of Resurrection, and so on, are matters which will only be sensed once physical death has actually occurred. It is said that God in His wisdom has deliberately deprived us of these experiences for the present, for we will come to know them in due time later on.

Another viewpoint is that all of the affairs that have been promised in the next life resemble our dreams when we are asleep. They are affairs of our imagination, and do not have a separate existence outside the imagination. For example, when we dream of a scorpion biting us, the scorpion has no physical existence, even though we may feel the pain of it to such a point that we wake up.

A third viewpoint is that all affairs relating to the next life are sensed according to the degree of development of the intellect, and so there will be varying degrees of comprehension among people.

Further, the meanings and secrets of the pleasures and pains of the next life can only be understood in this life as a metaphor. The joys that one experiences within the higher development of the intellect are a kind that no human eye has seen nor ear has heard, neither has such occurred in the heart of humankind.

But the affairs of the next life can only be truly understood by those whose faculty of the intellect is completely awakened – the realised ones. They are confirmed in their gnosis, and have combined both intellectual proof and inner certainty. They say the affairs of the next life are of absolute existence and certainty, and are far stronger and more complete, more firm and lasting, than anything we have experienced in this world. There is no comparison at all between their power and vividness and anything we may have experienced before in this world.

In summary, what we shall witness after this creation are essentially inner pictures which do not exist in this physical world of ours; nor can we truly feel or experience them by our present senses which are based on the physical realm. They exist in another world which has its own laws for sensing them.

The self, or soul, of each of those who are happy in the next life contains within it an incredible kingdom of unending dimensions and a world that is much vaster than whatever there is between the heavens and the earth. Those souls do not go beyond their own essence, but indeed, all that they own, all of their kingdom – the rivers, gardens, trees, pure companions and mansions – have arisen out of it. Those souls are actually the keepers of these wonders and the originators of all of it, by the permission and decree of the Creator.

So the final awakening and the images and pictures that come with it are so strong and powerful in their existence, so affecting in their trace, that they are more arresting and more powerful than anything one can experience in this world. A comparison between what one experiences and senses in the next creation with our present creation, is the difference between being suddenly but fully awake after being deeply asleep. That is the meaning of the Prophetic tradition, 'People are asleep, but when they die, they awake.'

Some people try to demonstrate that the next creation or consciousness is only spiritual in nature, and that there is no physical or material body involved with this return. The Prophetic teachings and the great gnostics affirm it is not a question of a material return – it is a question of another form, another dimension, another consciousness altogether.

Most of those who claim that the next creation is not of a material form are trying to prove that the next creation is based only on images. The great masters, Mulla Sadra, Ibn Arabi[9] and others say that it is a matter of even greater difference than what are called the 'images' and more remarkable than that. Nor does it matter what one calls it. It is an experience of another reality, another dimension and realm, beyond our power to describe adequately – more immediate, more powerful, more total and more arresting than anything we know in this life.

The journey of the self to the Garden of the next consciousness lies within our own existence – is in our essence. It is not something outside ourselves. The light that we see is not outside us. It is all part and parcel of one whole. It is totally interconnected by us, from us and to us, and we experience it that way after death, as we leave the body and enter the next consciousness.

Thus we have described how the self completes its journey in this life and begins its return towards its eternal source in the unseen.

4

Treatment, Cure and Fulfilment

In this chapter we shall examine the symptoms and conditions of the self and discuss their treatment, remedy and cure. We shall also discuss the meaning of virtues, examine the major vices of the self along with their root causes, and discuss their treatment and remedies.

In some Islamic teachings, the self is portrayed as essentially unchangeable. One cannot rid oneself completely of a certain natural disposition. Other teachings, however, analyse convincingly that people are inherently ingrained to accept the higher qualities and virtues, some more slowly than others.

The individual's basic natural self-tendencies are apparent from childhood, and generally these tendencies become established unless overcome by self-discipline. Their hold over the child prevails until such time as it begins to learn and apply corrective measures. The existence of these basic patterns or tendencies early on, and the subsequent task of gradually overcoming and disciplining them is part of the natural development of wisdom in humankind.

When the power of attraction to what is agreeable becomes developed in the child, its desires and its appetites become evident. Similarly, the power of repulsion of what is repugnant grows, and the child begins to resist and struggle against anything that it dislikes or anything which may obstruct the attainment of its desires.

As the power of discrimination grows in the child, intelligence and reasoning come into prominence. Soon self-discipline will begin to regulate behaviour such as appetite and irascibility. Such regulation will assist with the development of the higher intellect.

Discipline proceeds from the human desire and will to enlist the participation and assistance of the powers of attraction, repulsion and discrimination in its service. Nature is thus in the position of a master and teacher, in that it gives us the opportunity of learning what is of a virtuous nature and what is of a harmful nature by allowing us to experience it.

Virtue is primarily a matter of discipline as no one is created with a ready-made, developed understanding of virtue. We are born, however, with the seed of discrimination and of understanding virtues and vices. Virtue is the offspring of discipline.

We now turn to the importance of virtues to the self and examine the major virtues in greater detail.

The Virtues and the Self

The importance of virtues to self-development can be seen after defining what is meant by virtue. We define virtue as behaviour occurring at the centre of two extremes, both of which are unvirtuous. The virtuous value which is at the centre is not affected by unvirtuous values around it unless it moves towards one or the other extreme, away from the centre. When that happens, the virtue takes on the colour of that particular vice. For example, the virtue of generosity is the midpoint between two vices – meanness at one extreme, and indiscriminate giving, or wastefulness, at the other extreme.

This characteristic of virtue (lying at the centre between vices), becomes practically useful once understood, practised and perfected in actual life-transaction situations. Interacting and transaction with the extremes is an essential ingredient in acquiring the knowledge of virtues.

Virtues are the outcome of dynamic and active situations involving interaction with other people and beings. In our social exchanges, we will both teach and be taught virtues. Necessarily, we will have to be patient with all the afflictions and setbacks we experience until we perfect our knowledge.

Every tribe, society, culture and civilisation acknowledges virtues and vices, and humanity seems to be subconsciously and innately inclined to acknowledge and desire virtues and deplore vices.

As mentioned earlier, the two basic forces in life are the power of attraction, or desire, and the power of repulsion, or anger. All of our actions and behaviour stem ultimately from the force of these two motivations. When the power of repulsion reaches a state of balance and equilibrium with regard to its opposite attributes, of 'fight' on one extreme and 'flight' on the other, it emerges as the virtue of courage. Courage is the midpoint and the highest virtue or outcome of repulsion, or anger. Repulsion manifests in fight or flight.

The mature adult will manifest the various virtues emanating from the power of repulsion, such as fortitude, forbearance, greatness of spirit and so on, which will culminate in the ultimate virtue of courage, as we will see in the discussions that follow later.

The same applies for the power of attraction, or desire. Its opposite attributes are selfishness on one extreme and total abstemiousness on the other. When the power of attraction is in total equilibrium, the virtue that emerges at the centre of this equilibrium is modesty.

As the individual matures, we find that the extreme attributes, for example, of selfishness and total abstemiousness stabilise. This stabilisation arises out of the interaction that took place, and the growth of the rational self whose ultimate virtue is wisdom. As the awareness of the rational self increases regarding the power of attraction and the power of repulsion, it will lead to the process of developing and maturing an adult.

The Virtues and the Self according to al-Miskawayh

According to al-Miskawayh,[1] the self in its relationship to virtue can be defined as possessing four facets or aspects. He describes these four aspects as follows:

One is the bestial self, which is motivated by the power of attraction. If the bestial aspect is refined and purified as the self evolves, the highest virtue that will emerge is modesty or temperance. If the bestial self is not purified, it will fall towards its lowest vice, indulgence, the opposite of modesty.

The second aspect is the predatory self, which is motivated by the power of repulsion. If the predatory self is refined and purified, the highest virtue that it will attain as we have seen is courage. If the predatory self is not refined, it will fall to its lowest or opposite vice of cowardice.

The third aspect is the rational self. If the movement of the rational self is towards its highest virtue, it will attain wisdom. But if it moves to the lowest base tendencies of the self, it will remain in ignorance.

The fourth aspect is the combined virtues. When the three highest virtues of modesty, courage and wisdom combine, the outcome results in the ultimate virtue of all – justice. Its lowest opposite extreme is injustice, or oppression.

We will now examine the major virtues arising from the four aspects of the self in greater detail.

The Bestial Self

When the bestial self reaches its highest evolvement, it achieves modesty or temperance. Modesty is self-restraint in conduct and expression. It is a virtue that manifests when one conforms to sound discrimination so that one is not led by passions and is thus not enslaved by them.

From modesty comes the virtue of chastity, or shame, which is defined as self-restraint from committing bad deeds, thereby avoiding blame and justified insults.

After chastity comes tranquillity or steadfastness. This is defined as the tranquillity of the self when desires arise.

Following tranquillity comes the virtue of patience, or self-control, which is defined as restraining the self so as not to chase after desires or pleasures.

Then comes the virtue of liberality, which is defined as keeping to the middle path in giving and taking, and spending on what is right, with the right amount and in the right manner.

Next comes integrity, which is a virtue of the self which makes it acquire wealth in the right way, give it in the right way and abstain from acquiring it in any wrong way.

Then comes sobriety, which is defined as moderation in food, drink and adornment.

Then follows benignity, which is the disposition towards what is praiseworthy, and zeal to accomplish the good.

It is followed by the virtue of self-discipline, which is judging things rightly and arranging them in the proper way.

Next comes the virtue of good disposition which is defined as complementing the self with beautiful adornment.

Then comes mildness, which is the quietude which comes to the self from an innate aptitude that is free from perturbation.

Next is steadiness, which is defined as the tranquillity and stability of the self during agitations which tend to arise.

And finally comes the virtue of piety, which is defined as the constant performance of good deeds leading to perfection of the self.

We have seen that the highest virtue to which the bestial self's energy can give rise is modesty, and that it is virtue that lies between the two extreme vices of indulgence on the one hand and total abstemiousness, or the death of all desire, on the other. Miskawayh defines indulgence as running headlong into everything that gives pleasure, simply for the sake of experiencing all those pleasures. Abstemiousness, however, does not include abstention from the pursuit of legitimate pleasures which the body needs for its normal functioning and which are permitted by law and reason.

A complete list of the virtues of modesty and those which follow from it can be found in the chart of virtues according to Miskawayh (see Table 1 on p. 114). A list of a number of the vices which relate to these virtues is included in the chart, and where these are not included, the reader can recognise them for himself. If the exact or appropriate name for all of these is not found, it would not be difficult at least to understand their meanings.

The Predatory Self

The predatory self's highest virtue is that of courage. When the power of repulsion (anger) and its characteristics (the 'lion tendency' in us) is refined, stabilised and tempered, courage emerges. Courage is an attribute of redressing an imbalance, and hence relates to justice. Courage is at the centre of two vices – cowardice and recklessness. The following virtues stem from courage:

First, greatness of spirit, which is being prepared for significant or important affairs and yet minimising them in one's own eyes. It is also defined as nobility of spirit.

The second virtue is intrepidity. This is defined as confidence in the face of fearful events, to the extent that no despair can ever overwhelm one.

Third is composure, defined as the means by which one can calmly endure happiness, sorrow and other afflictions, even the moment of death itself.

Then comes fortitude which is defined as the strength of the self to bear pain and to resist it, especially in dangerous situations.

The next virtue is forbearance, and is defined as the ability to remain tranquil and keep from being angered easily or quickly.

Next is self-containment or self-control, and it is the ability to restrain movement or action at moments of serious consequence.

Next is what is called manliness, which is defined as the aspiration to perform great deeds in expectation of a goodly outcome.

Then comes endurance which is defined as the ability or capacity to use the faculties of the body in a consistent manner for what is good, through discipline and good habits (see Table 2 on p. 115).

The Rational Self

The evolvement of the rational self occurs when it follows the prescribed path of divine guidance and avoids the pitfalls of the lower self.

The ultimate virtue of one's obedience and acceptance of divine reality is wisdom and knowledge. Wisdom is the knowledge of things divine and human, which gives discrimination concerning which of several possible actions should be performed, and which should be avoided. It is the midpoint between stupidity on the one hand and impudence, or the deliberate suppression of wisdom, on the other. From wisdom come the following virtues:

Intelligence, the quick grasp of concepts and the self's ready understanding of them, is the virtue at midpoint between cunning at one extreme and dullness at the other.

Retention is the persistence of the images of what is derived by the mind or imagination, and is the virtue between attentiveness (to what should not be remembered) and forgetfulness (or neglect of what should be remembered).

Rationality, the conformity of a sound investigation of objects to what they are, is the median between frivolity (or going too far in the consideration of an object until one is led beyond what it actually is), and imbecility (or the failure to consider an object sufficiently for what it is).

Next is clarity of understanding, which is the readiness of the self to deduce what is required. It is the median between quick flashes of ideas that prevent deducing what is necessary, and slowness of deduction.

Excellence and strength of understanding mean the ability to contemplate what follows from the antecedent. It is the virtue between excessive contemplation, which leads away from it to something else, and deficient contemplation which falls short of the necessary consequence.

The next virtue is the capacity for learning, which is a strength of the mind and a sharpness of understanding by which theoretical matters are apprehended. It is the virtue at midpoint between the ability to learn with such ease that it is not retained by the mind, and finding learning too difficult, or impossible (see Table 3 on p. 116).

The Combined Virtues

When the three virtues of wisdom, courage and modesty are combined in the self, the outcome that results is the highest virtue of all, justice (see Table 4 on p. 117).

Justice is a virtue which causes one to be fair to oneself and to others, by refraining from giving a greater portion of that which is useful to oneself and less to others, and less of that which is harmful to oneself and more to others. The just man applies equality, which is a proportionate relation between things, and it is from this meaning that the virtue of justice is derived. Justice is the midpoint between the extremes of doing injustice to others, and suffering injustice from others or from oneself.

The virtues which derive from justice are friendship, harmony, family fellowship, recompense, fair play, honest dealing, amicability and devotion.

We note that all of man's experiences of vice and virtue have been created to help him to evolve along the path of higher virtues, by avoiding the extreme vices on either side and remaining in the centre, where one virtue leads to a higher virtue. Through this dynamic unfolding, one comes to recognise the ways in which to avoid damage or harm and to achieve well-being and stable happiness.

The Tree of Virtues

A similar system of classifying virtues can be illustrated by drawing the tree of virtues. We read the tree of virtues as follows: the ultimate and highest fruit of each branch is to be found at the trunk of the tree, near its root. See Figure 1.

For example, if we examine the power of repulsion, we find the highest and most important virtue that the power of repulsion can ultimately bring about is courage. So courage is to be found at the trunk, because it is the potentially highest fruit of repulsion.

The ultimate potential present at the root is the source, and that potential leads to other virtues that the mature adult will develop as he or she evolves towards the ultimate virtue of real courage. All the virtues, however, interact in order to produce courage.

Further Comments on Virtues

A special distinction is to be made here between true human virtues and other attributes that only resemble virtues, according to the ethical philosopher Tusi. [2]

For example, Tusi speaks of the courage of the lion, the elephant and other animals. Although their behaviour resembles human courage, it is not the same. The lion is innately confident in its own strength and superiority, and readily imagines its own victory. Moreover, in many cases, his quarry is quite devoid of any instrument of real resistance. In relation to his prey, the lion may be compared to a fully armed warrior attacking an unarmed weakling. These are not conditions in which we consider behaviour to be virtuous or praiseworthy.

The truly courageous man is a person whose wariness of committing anything foul or abominable exceeds any fear of threat or danger to his life, for which reason he prefers a just death to a reprehensible life.

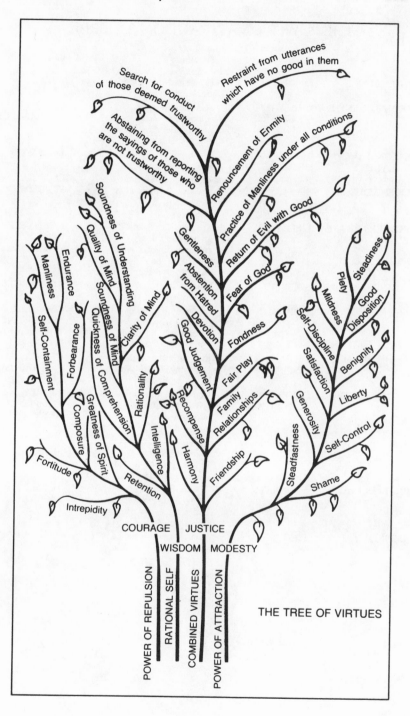

THE TREE OF VIRTUES

THE POWER OF ATTRACTION (DESIRE)

Vice	Virtue	Definition	Vice
INDULGENCE	MODESTY	Self-restraint in conduct and expression.	TOTAL ABSTENTION
SHAMELESSNESS	CHASTITY/ SHAME	Self-restraint from committing misdeeds, thereby avoiding blame and justified insults.	EXCESSIVE BASHFULNESS
INCONSTANCY/ VOLATILITY	TRANQUILLITY/ STEADFASTNESS	Tranquillity of the self when desires arise.	INDIFFERENCE
UNRESTRAINT/ LICENTIOUSNESS	PATIENCE/ SELF-CONTROL	Restraining of the self, so as not to chase after desires and pleasures.	EXCESSIVE RIGIDITY
INDISCRIMINATE/ EXTRAVAGANCE	LIBERALITY	Keeping the mean in giving and taking, and spending for what is right, in the right amount, in the right manner.	MEANNESS/ DENYING ONE'S DUE
IMMODERATION	SOBRIETY	Moderation in food, drink and adornment.	ABSTEMIOUS–NESS
MALIGNANCY	BENIGNITY	Disposition towards what is praiseworthy and zeal to accomplish the good.	OBSEQUIOUS-NESS/TRYING TOO HARD TO PLEASE
UNDISCIPLINED	SELF-DISCIPLINE	Judging things rightly and arranging things in the proper way.	OVERLY FASTIDIOUS
BAD DISPOSITION	GOOD DISPOSITION	Complementing the self with beautiful adornment (in moderation).	OVERLY COMPLIMENT-ARY
PERTURBATION	MILDNESS	Quietude which comes to the self from an innate aptitude that is free from perturbation.	EXCESSIVE MEEKNESS
INSTABILITY	STEADINESS	Tranquillity and stability of the soul during the agitation which tends to arise in the pursuit of desires.	TOTALLY PASSIVE
IMPIETY	PIETY	Constant performance of good deeds which leads to perfection of the self.	ASCETICISM

Table 1

THE POWER OF REPULSION (ANGER)

Vice	Virtue	Definition	Vice
COWARDICE	COURAGE	Applying good judgement in confronting dangerous situations: namely, that one should not fear alarming things if to perform them is good or to withstand them is commendable.	RECKLESS-NESS/ FOLLY
PETTINESS	GREATNESS OF SPIRIT/ MAGNANIMITY	Preparedness for significant or great affairs, yet minimising them in one's own eyes.	ARROGANCE
DESPAIR	INTREPIDITY	Confidence in the face of fearful events, to the extent that no despair can overwhelm one.	OVER CONFIDENCE/ FOOL-HARDINESS
DISHEVELMENT	COMPOSURE	The means by which the self can endure calmly happiness, sadness and other afflictions, even the moment of death itself.	UNCARING/ INDIFFERENCE
OVERLY SUBMISSIVE	FORTITUDE	Courage in adversity, and the strength of the self to bear pain and to resist it, especially in dangerous situations.	MASOCHISM
QUICK TO ANGER	FORBEARANCE	To remain tranquil and keep from becoming angered easily.	DOCILE
UNDISCI-PLINED	SELF-CONTROL/ SELF-CONTAINMENT	Ability to restrain from movement or action in moments of serious consequences.	EXCESSIVE RIGIDITY
APATHY	MANLINESS	The aspiration to perform great deeds in expectation of a goodly outcome.	MACHISMO
LACK OF ENDURANCE	ENDURANCE	The ability to use the faculties of the body for what is good through discipline and good habits.	OVER EXTENSION OF BODILY ORGANS

Table 2

THE RATIONAL SELF

Vice	Virtue	Definition	Vice
STUPIDITY (i.e., deliberate suppression of wisdom)	WISDOM	The knowledge of things divine and human, which gives discrimination to which of possible actions should be performed and which should be avoided	IMPUDENCE (i.e., use of rational faculty for wrong ends)
DULLNESS	INTELLIGENCE	The quick flaring of conclusions and the soul's easy understanding of them.	CUNNING
FORGETFUL-NESS (neglecting what should be remembered)	RETENTION	The persistence of the images of what is derived by the mind or the imagination.	ATTENTIVE-NESS (to what should not be remembered)
IMBECILITY (failure to consider an object sufficiently for what it is)	RATIONALITY	The conformity of a sound investigation of objects to what they are.	FRIVOLITY (going too far in consider-ation, until one is led beyond what it is)
SLOWNESS OF DEDUCTION	CLARITY OF UNDERSTANDING	The readiness of the self to deduce what is required.	MENTAL FLASHES (which prevent deducing what is required)
DEFICIENT CONTEMPLATION (which falls short of the necessary consequence)	EXCELLENCE & STRENGTH OF UNDERSTANDING	Contemplation of what follows from the antecedent.	EXCESSIVE CONTEMPLATION (which leads away from it to something else)
FINDING LEARNING TOO DIFFICULT	CAPACITY FOR LEARNING	The strength of the mind and sharpness of understanding by which theoretical matters are apprehended.	LEARNING WITH SUCH EASE (that it does not remain fixed in the mind)

Table 3

THE COMBINED VIRTUES

Vice	Virtue	Definition
INJUSTICE	JUSTICE	When the three virtues of Wisdom, Courage & Modesty combine in moderation one with another, they result in the highest virtue of all, which is Justice.
ENMITY	FRIENDSHIP	Sincere love which causes one to take interest in all that concerns one's friends and to choose to do all the good that one can for them.
DISHARMONY	HARMONY	The agreement of opinions and beliefs brought about by close contact leading to cooperation in the daily affairs of life.
LACK OF KINSHIP	FAMILY FELLOWSHIP	Sharing the goods of this world with one's relations.
NON-ACKNOWLEDGE-MENT TO OTHERS	RECOMPENSE	Repayment of a charitable gift, with its equivalent or more.
FOUL PLAY	FAIR PLAY	To give and take in business equitably, with fairness and according to the interests of all concerned.
DISHONEST TRANSACTION	HONEST DEALING	To recompense without regret or reminding others of favours done to them.
ESTRANGEMENT	AMICABILITY	The desire to win the affections of the deserving and the virtuous with a pleasing disposition and performance of deeds which inspire such affection.
INFIDELITY	PIETY	In honour, glorification and obedience of God in revering His favourite ones: the angels, the Prophets, the Imams (Masters of the Prophetic House) and following the commands of the Law.

Table 4

The Islamic heritage presents us with a beautiful description of the true meaning of courage. The Arabic word *jihad* is derived from the root which means to endeavour, strive, expend energy or resist. *Jihad* is to fight against evil for the sake of truth. It implies an act of support of reality against falsehood.

The person who does not carry out his duty of expressed courage (*jihad*) under these circumstances will thereafter live out an oppressed and distasteful life. The days won from death are miserable and troubled. He passes the days in contempt and humiliation, hostility and reproach. Hence, the truly virtuous man would rather expedite death with courage than extend life with dishonour, tribulation and shame.

Tusi distinguishes between courage, recklessness and indiscrimination, and warns against people who have no fear of losing honour, or bringing shame to modesty, or who are unafraid of perilous situations, of violent earthquakes, thunderbolts, or chronic diseases or painful ailments, or the loss of companions, family or friends, or catastrophes and the like. These people who have no fear are closer to madness and impudence than they are to courage.

There are incidents which appear courageous but are not. There are people, for example, basically in situations of safety and leisure who cast themselves into dangerous situations, like jumping from a high cliff or over a great waterfall, deliberately exposing themselves to danger. These people are merely seeking sensation, excitement and stimulation. They are not courageous in the true sense. Their actions are more closely related to vainglory and folly.

Tusi does not consider suicide (which is forbidden in Islam) under any condition to be an act of courage. Rather, it is an act of cowardice. It is the ultimate flight from things undesirable.

Vengeance is often held to be a virtue, but it is only so if undertaken in accordance with the definition of courage.

Tusi notes that not every continent or courageous man is wise; but every wise man is both continent and courageous.

Further Comments on Justice

Tusi also expounds upon the virtue of justice. Among the virtues, as we have already seen, none is more perfect than that of justice. The final balance and point of equilibrium is justice, and all else is peripheral to it.

In most of our material transactions, we find the just arbitrator or mediator in the exchange balance is currency. So if an exchange between two parties does not or cannot come about through the justice of money alone (money being the silent arbitration element), then a rationally just person is sought, as mediator who can establish the proper order and arrange an exchange.

The preservation of justice among men cannot be upheld without three things: divine commandment (divinely revealed laws and knowledge), human arbitration (the just, rational and impartial being) and a medium of exchange (such as money).

Money or its equivalent is required for the reason that without it, negotiation in various transactions would be exceedingly difficult. (How many eggs for example, would equal a new roof?)

Aristotle said that justice is not a part of virtue but is all virtues in their entirety, while tyranny or oppression, the opposite of justice, is not a part of vice but all vices in their entirety.

Man-made laws try to curtail human greed and other lower tendencies and vices in a limited and artificial manner, whereas divinely revealed laws allow for these lower tendencies and vices to find an expression (and a cure) within acceptable limits.

According to Tusi, justice in a broad sense is due in three respects: towards reality – which a person must perform in respect of what is due to his Creator; towards humanity – which a person must perform in respect of the rights of his fellow man; and, finally, exercising the proper courtesy towards oneself.

In the final analysis, justice cannot be performed unless the faculty of reasoning controls and directs the senses. An angry person, or one who is given to excessive appetites or quarrelsomeness, acts by whims and fancies without consulting reason. Such a person only brings about disruption and chaos, and cannot dispense justice.

In conclusion, Tusi states that it is incumbent upon the rational individual to apply justice within one's own self by the proper utilisation of one's own faculties and in the development of proper habits. If he does not do this, then appetite or desire will move him to something consonant with its own nature – such as indulgence and anger – both of which are opposed to just behaviour. When that happens we seek all manner of appetitive gratification in all kinds of sudden impulses. The result of the ensuing upheaval is always harmful as well as unjust, to oneself and others.

We now turn to a discussion on the treatment and cure of the self.

The Treatment and Cure of the Self

In physical treatment, the modern doctor examines and recognises the state of his patient, and considers the causes and effects in order to understand the nature and root of the illness. We have a similar situation in the treatment of the self, its symptoms, conditions and vices. Such treatment is often termed spiritual medicine. According to Islamic teachings, we must also observe natural cause and effect, to understand how these vices occur and how to overcome them. Ultimately, all treatment of the self depends on removal of the root source of these vices.

Ultimately, all vices occur because of ignorance in oneself, for ignorance is the veiling of knowledge. If there is no ignorance, one will easily understand the cause of his symptoms. Having become aware of the source of the condition, the treatment will have already begun, for recognition of its source is the beginning of the cure.

According to the rule of opposites, any condition is a symptom of a disturbed or imbalanced state, and the extent of any condition is its distance from equilibrium. Its cure therefore lies in the application of its opposite. The cure occurs when neutralisation takes place and balance is restored.

When and how to apply the remedy is entirely dependent upon the discretion of the qualified individual who is applying it. In the beginning, it may be difficult to overcome the inertia, but once a start is made, the momentum of the cure must be speeded up, regularised and habitualised. When the benefits of the treatment begin to appear and the advantages of new habits and the disadvantages of old ones are realised, then recovery is on its way. The new, pleasant taste will be attractive and the former unpleasant taste repulsive, and thus one is propelled forward by both of these forces towards a cure.

Initially, one requires qualified help to restore one's health, and with suffering and education we learn to avoid in future what brings about these conditions of imbalance and disturbance. With increased knowledge and self-awareness, we may ourselves bring about the remedy for our condition, for ultimately, wherein lies the illness also lies the cure.

Treating the conditions of the self is not always by applying its opposite. It is frequently by removal of the tarnishing. Our purpose is to educate and groom the self and not to break it or shatter the ego. If we eradicate the self, we have eradicated the being, for beingness is centred around the self. All that we want is to make the self crystallise along the pattern of its higher nature – the spirit – which is a hologram of the original untarnished state of unity, infinity, limitless freedom and the highest state of attainment.

In the case of spiritual progress, the dangers and pitfalls are more complex. Recognition and contentment with progress itself could be one of the greatest barriers to further spiritual unfoldment. Only a pure mirror can reflect unblemished light, and the heart of a seeker will often miss seeing distortions and could easily be misled despite the best of intentions and hard work. Only those who have arrived know how treacherous this subtle business is, and how unlikely arrival is without the reference points of the masters of this art.

The Three Major Sources of the Conditions of the Self

According to Tusi, the major sources of the conditions of the self are rooted in the three primary forces or powers that propel the human self.

The primary forces which direct the actions of the self are the power of attraction, or desire; the power of repulsion, or anger; and the power of discrimination, or reasoning. Disorder in either the quantity or quality of any of these forces is the root cause of any adverse condition. Disorders arise as a result of either an excess, a neglect or a perversion of any of these powers, and manifest themselves as various symptoms and conditions.

The major sources of symptoms of each of the three primary forces can be described in outline form as follows:

1. The power of attraction, when in a state of (a) excess, manifests itself as envy and its various forms of greed, gluttony, passion, and lust for persons and objects that are not appropriate to it. In a state of (b) neglect, it manifests itself in sloth, in being too languid to seek sustenance, in being incapable of carrying on one's own life, and in sluggishness of appetite. In a state of (c) perversion, it manifests itself as indulgence, relish in consuming or eating corrupt, unnourishing things, and in all aspects of perverted sexuality, such as homosexuality and all use of appetite outside the natural laws.

2. The power of repulsion, when in a state of (a) excess, manifests itself in anger, violent rage, vindictiveness, unfounded jealousy, and so on. In a state of (b) neglect, manifests itself in cowardice, lack of self-regard, general weakness in one's nature, and faint-heartedness. When in a state of (c) perversion, it manifests itself as fear, and yearning for perverse or unjust revenge.

3. The power of discrimination, when in a state of (a) excess, manifests itself as perplexity, being troubled, or as a showing guile, cleverness or too much ingenuity. When in a state of (b) neglect, it manifests itself as simple ignorance, foolishness, stupidity, inadequacy and inability to speculate or discern. In a state of (c) perversion, it manifests itself as compounded ignorance, as a yearning for knowledge which does not assist in the development and perfecting of the self and in seeking irrelevant information and facts that are no use for self-development.

Although we speak frequently of the body and the self as though they were separate, this is only for the sake of discussion and understanding. The fact is that the human self is attached to its corporeal frame until the actual separation of one from the other upon death. When either is affected in some way, such an effect necessarily produces a change in the other, for the two are very closely linked and related, as we know.

Thus when the self is affected by excesses of anger, passion or constant grief, this state necessarily brings about a change in the body in all sorts of ways. Some changes, for example, are clearly visible, such as agitation, trembling, emaciation and so forth.

Likewise, whenever the body is directly affected by illness – especially when these occur in a superior part of the body, such as the heart or brain – these necessarily bring about a change in the state of the self.

This being the case, one who wishes to treat the self must first endeavour to find out if there has been any change in the physical constitution. Should physical disturbances be present, the appropriate treatment must be administered. If, on the other hand, it is the self as such which is directly afflicted, without any obvious effect upon the physical frame, then one must look to the discipline of spiritual remedies.

Conditions of the Power of Attraction

The most severe of the conditions of attraction, or desire, as we have mentioned, are the following: envy, which arises out of excess; sloth, which arises out of neglect; and indulgence, which arises out of perversion.

1. *Envy*. Envy arises when the power of attraction in the self reaches a point of excess and manifests itself as greed, gluttony, passion, and lust for persons and objects that are not appropriate or conducive to one's state of well-being. An excess of greed causes one to wish to be graced with the advantages, achievements and possessions of other people, without having gone through the process of earning them. The aspiration of the envious person is to remove these advantages from others and attract them to himself. Yet the fortunes of others are the direct result of the interaction of countless variables that are particular to the individual being and cannot be earned, gained or possessed without experiencing or being subjected to those circumstances. The envious person covets the fruits of that experience without being willing or able to engage in the process that leads to them. It is therefore based on ignorance of the unified nature of reality.

The origin of this vice is in the compounding of ignorance and avidity: ignorance of the fact that the outcome is only going to satisfy us temporarily, and avidity which reflects the basic insecurity of our nature. For it is quite out of the question for one person to hope to amass all of the worldly goods and possessions and achievements of all other beings. Even if such a possibility were to occur, the avid, envious person would derive no satisfaction from it, for by one's very nature new desires will continue to arise as long as one lives. The envious must also be made to see that one's avidity can never be satisfied by things designed to feed the lower self, which by its nature is insatiable. The appetite of envy can never be filled. Therefore the outcome of the state of envy can only be grief and suffering.

Envy has been described[3] as the most abominable and odious of conditions. Odious is the person who wishes to have harm befall his enemy, and more harmful still is he who wishes harm to befall someone who is not even his enemy. So the condition of envy is the most abominable of all, and consequently one is always grief-stricken, for such a person can only seek to overcome distress at the expense of others, that is, by acquiring the good of others.

The most destructive of all kinds of envy is that which occurs among people of intellect, as it is a very subtle and deep illness. It is that type of envy which is directed against other people of wisdom and their gaining in knowledge.

To overcome envy, one needs to reflect upon the fact that envy is the result of ignorance of the nature of reality. To consider the total position, both negative and positive, of the person who is envied could rationally reveal to the envious one how whimsical and illogical his mental state is. If one is envious of another's wealth, for example, a brief consideration of how that wealth was obtained could illustrate how untenable one's desire is. That wealth could have been obtained by inheritance, which one cannot emulate. If, on the other hand, one considers the hard work, commitment and many sacrifices that may have gone into acquiring that wealth, and one is willing and able to make those same commitments and emulate them, then it is no longer envy, and it becomes a positive objective that one can strive toward. Inherent in envy is a falsehood of premise which needs to be investigated. Once found, one is released from envy.

We need to differentiate between envy and emulation. Emulation is a desire to acquire a noble quality or a desired object belonging to another, without any wish for its removal from that person. Emulation, moreover, is of two kinds: one is praiseworthy and one is reprehensible. Praiseworthy emulation occurs when the longing is directed towards acquiring various felicities and virtues. Reprehensible emulation is when the longing is directed to the baser appetites or pleasures. The same is true for avidity – it, too, can be directed either towards virtues or to worthless or harmful objectives.

2. *Sloth*. Sloth is based generally on two things: fear of change, and lack of positively regarded experiences.

Fear of change is fear of active and dynamic situations. Such situations necessarily involve a host of changing and therefore challenging factors – such as making decisions, being questioned and judged, and the possibility of failure – all of which can be avoided through sloth. Inimical to such challenges is the bitterness of potential disappointment, and therefore affliction and suffering. The person fearful of such exposure retreats through inactivity into the stagnation of sloth.

But sloth is concomitantly rooted in the lack of tasting and experiencing the positive aspects of living in this world and growing in knowledge; of developing outwardly – materially and socially – and inwardly, in inner awakenings and unfoldment.

The condition of a slothful person is like a man who is asleep. To awaken him, we use whatever measure – a gentle nudge, a hard tug, a bucket of water – will bring about a response. At the physical level, diet and exercise are essential ingredients, to be prescribed appropriately. One needs to be motivated to achieve health and, at other levels, to develop love for achievement or discovery. It could be sympathy or compassion for others which could bring about a positive energy in a person and cause him to act and overcome his sloth. It could be anger against injustice which could move him out of a condition of sloth, by taking on some activity against injustice.

The key is to find the right motivating factor which is appropriate at the time, and that can only be what touches the person and concerns him. What is important is to find the right hook – which can seem insignificant at first.

Then comes the development of an appetite for life and worldly joys. Consideration of the natural laws, beauty and other things can all be used as an attraction to enable the healthy energies of life to flow into the slothful one. After all, the interaction with life comes about either through basic physical needs or from the love of knowledge and inner discovery. One way or another, we need to be propelled into the dynamics of life, where learning and growth take place.

3. *Indulgence*. The third condition of attraction is indulgence in all that is despicable, which arises out of perversion. That perversion is in allowing the reins on behaviour to be taken away from the higher self and given to the destructive carelessness of the lower self. Giving way to the excesses of the lower tendencies and desires manifests itself as relish in consuming corrupt, unnourishing things, in all aspects of perverted sexuality and in all uses of appetite beyond the natural laws. There is no end to indulgence once one is fully immersed in it.

The treatment is based on abstinence. A complete abstinence extracts that patient from the state of indulgence, so that weaning can take place. If indulgence has reached such a point that a person has been put completely out of balance in his physical or inner state and is thoroughly immersed in it, then the only cure is total and utter severance from these indulgences. If it is moderate, then a cure may be effected by redressing the balance gradually until one is weaned off these baser tendencies.

Whatever appropriate measure is taken to enable the indulgent to recognise the benefits of his abstinence, it needs to open new horizons to compensate for what appears to be a restriction in the process of weaning him off his gluttony. The benefits in the form of better health, increased general well-being and greater energy are all conducive to better performance in other and new activities. Restriction, accompanied by the realisation of the benefits from restriction, is the start of the curing process.

Summary

These three conditions related to the power of attraction are a result of neglecting the lower self instead of disciplining it, training it and leading it towards higher planes. However, basically all treatment of the lower self depends upon removal of the vices.

If a person allows the appetites and desires to rule over the self, one could end up in a worse state than the lowest of the animals. Once the self is obsessed by these desires, nothing can bring about lasting satisfaction, and its behaviour will therefore be erratic and unstable.

One difference between the lower self of the human and the animal is that most animals in their natural habitat behave within general limits and will be satiated whereas the human being knows no limits. It starts with one thing which leads to another, and is never satisfied as it increases in its appetites and desires.

Also with human desire, we notice that it can shift from one direction to another. For example, love of beauty could lead to the love of collecting objects of beauty and art, or the love of gazing upon a beautiful face could end up in love of intercourse and so on; unlike the animal, where the appetites are much more basic and simple.

Another difference is that whereas the animal satisfies its appetite without thought or worry, the human being in satisfying his desire is always coloured with fears and anxieties about them. It is stated in the Qur'an:

> Satan [i.e. the lower self] has been made an enemy
> of you, so take him as such. (35:6)

It is related in a tradition that the Prophet said, 'For every human being there is a Satan.' He also said, 'Satan flows in the veins of all human beings, so he [i.e. our lower negative tendencies] affects all human beings.' This implies that Satan manifests himself through our lower nature and baser actions. In another tradition, the Prophet also said, 'God has helped me with my Satan [i.e. lower self], and it has submitted.'

So the remedy to control and elevate the lower self is by disciplining it, training it and leading it to the higher self.

The first and foremost remedy to stop the rampage of the lower self is to reduce its strength by restricting its fodder or fuel, in the sense of food, drink and all other physical gratifications. Restriction of diet and fasting increases sensitivity and awareness by means of which better balance and control can be achieved.

The second remedy is to weigh the self with greater disci

pline in order to train and encourage it in obedience so that
it may be subservient with insight to rationality and correct
thinking.

The third is to elevate the self by calling upon and turning towards the higher self. By doing so, one will learn
the deep meaning of true submission and dependence upon
reality.

If these three remedies are combined, it will be much
easier for the self to be weaned of its baser elements, and to
be enriched with its potential higher virtues.

The Conditions of the Power of Repulsion

The most severe of the conditions of repulsion, according
to Tusi, are these three: anger, which arises out of excess;
cowardice, which arises out of neglect; and fear, which
arises out of perversion.

Anger

Anger derives from an excess of the force of repulsion, and
manifests itself as rage, vindictiveness and the like.

The principal force behind anger is the appetite for vengeance, as suggested earlier. So forceful is the appetite for
vengeance that one of our masters said that among the most
difficult of actions is to have compassion and clemency
when wrong has been done to one.

When the desire for revenge becomes uncontrollable, the
fire of rage is ignited. The blood begins to seethe and the
brain and arteries are excited and heated. That is why, in
early Sufi writings, anger has been called a dark vapour.
The intelligence is cut off as if by a veil, and its controlling
influence over action grows feeble. The body becomes like
a cave in a mountain, inside which a fire rages. Nothing
can be seen except dense smoke and blackness. So the
senses and higher faculties cannot in any way guide or
control, or point to a way out once rage takes over. While
this state lasts, it is virtually impossible to treat the sensory
deterioration or to extinguish the blaze, for everything that
is normally used to deal with an incipient conflagration now
becomes the very fuel of its energy – indeed, the reason for its
increase. If one rebukes or reproves rage, it only flares more

intensely. If one resorts to placation, the burning brands simply multiply.

Naturally, the situation differs somewhat from one case to another and from one individual to the next, according to his or her constitution and type. Some people's constitutions resemble sulphur and ignite at the smallest spark; while others are like oil, which requires a greater cause to ignite, while still others are like dry wood, which takes more time to ignite and is easier to put out. Others have constitutions like wet wood, very much more difficult to ignite and fairly easy to extinguish.

One can extend these metaphors and examples until one reaches the case of the person who is almost impossible to ignite. At the other extreme, as we have at times experienced, there is the person with whom even the slightest cause, a mere word, produces the most volatile explosion.

Extreme rages within the self are worse than the case of a ship on the high seas during a typhoon. It is actually easier to bring such a ship to safety because there are people at work on board who are actively interested in reducing the danger and possibility of drowning, whereas a person who is full of rage has cut himself off from the senses that could prevail and control the rage.

Ali ibn Abi Talib has said that anger or vehemence is a kind of madness whose author can only have regrets, and if he does not acknowledge these regrets, then that madness becomes firmly established.

If anger is not acknowledged and dealt with, it can choke off the warmth of the heart, producing sicknesses which will only lead ultimately to destruction. The warmth of the heart means the normal pulse of life in a man's breast, which is its real function. We do not describe a furiously angry man as possessing a warm, supple or moving heart while he is angry.

Tusi provides a list of the major causes of anger: conceit, pride, contention, quarrelsomeness, jesting, arrogance, scorn, treachery, unfairness, and acquisitiveness.

At the centre of many, if not all, of the foregoing is the yearning for revenge.

(a) Conceit. Conceit (i.e. self-love or self-glorification) is to lie about oneself. It is the false imagination which causes a person to lie about one's own situation or rank. The more one knows about oneself, the more one finds weaknesses.

Those who care to develop the self dwell upon rectifying shortcomings, rather than being content with existing characteristics (which may or may not be virtuous). In any case, specific virtues cannot be taken in isolation. One cannot congratulate oneself about one or a few virtues one possesses while the rest of the self is riddled with vice and harmful and non-virtuous actions.

It is related in one of the Prophetic traditions that a person will certainly perish whenever he has conceit, and whenever he considers that he has many good actions. Another tradition relates that there is no loneliness worse than being conceited.

When the self becomes aware of its own faults, shortcomings and deficiencies, and recognises that virtue is potentially attainable by all humanity, then we can overcome conceit. The treatment of conceit in other words lies in making it a practice to see one's own faults, to admit one's shortcomings, and to recognise and mention the good qualities of others.

(b) Pride. Pride is vainglory in external things, and takes many forms. Pride in one's lineage – in one's own ancestors – is one form. If that person's virtuous ancestors were here today, it might be pointed out that the proud descendant in fact possesses none of the virtues or qualities the family was renowned for, and hence is basing his pride on what does not belong to him. The descendant may have spoken the truth about his ancestors, but may also be testifying to how poorly they handed down their virtues. A tradition relates that the Prophet said, 'Do not bring me your genealogies, but show me your own virtuous actions.'

Another form of pride is in the possession of beautiful objects and adornments, jewellery, clothing and so on; also, one's ability to perform well, whether with efficiency, agility or speed. Here in any case the superiority lies in the body, its skills or possessions, obviously not in the self.

Once one realises that everything that is external or physical is impermanent and subject to decay, one would appreciate through that knowledge that there can be no permanence or stability in what one has based one's pride on, and thereby the cause of pride is removed. The remedy lies in constantly bringing one to that state of awareness until one is able truly to recognise and accept the truth of it.

A practical remedy is to see oneself as being smaller and less than other people at all times. By practising humility, pride can gradually be removed. Specific remedies for this can be found in a later section on Arrogance.

(c) Contention and (d) Quarrelsomeness. Contention and quarrelsomeness are both based on discord and disharmony, and are therefore aspects of ignorance. These two vices cause intimacy and friendship to disappear, producing instead repulsion, separation, dislike, hostility and ultimately destruction and breakdown, for the entire world and its functions and the universe itself depend on familiarity, love, harmony and unity.

Quarrelsomeness is among those basic corruptions that disrupt the order of the universe. As such, it is one of the most abhorred and destructive of vices. Engaging in contention or quarrelsomeness is to preserve one's own position while attacking another's. It is essentially destructive and negative.

The manner of resolving a dispute is as important as the reason for it. Quarrelsomeness only brings about greater anger, which in turn casts veil upon veil over ignorance. Instead of illuminating the heart of the matter, the darkness of ignorance is reinforced. It must therefore be stopped. The remedy is to bite one's tongue. Simply not to reply. Silence.

This treatment requires awareness and insight. The remedy can occur if one does not cling to a fixed image of oneself and one's position and reputation. Once a person sees that what one is doing is causing greater discord and dispersion, then the process of reduction and of an eventual end to one's pugnacious ways may occur. With that realisation, one will only respond if it is of help or positive benefit to another, and if it upholds justice. This positive response will neutralise the contention, whereupon clarity will prevail and all will benefit.

(e) Jesting. Jesting may be employed as a means of restoring equilibrium or as a corrective measure. We may sometimes want to say something in a manner that sweetens the message somewhat and we employ jest for this purpose. So used, the behaviour is praiseworthy. It is related that the prophets used jest, but not to play the fool or mock. Their jesting was all in truth and for a good purpose.

When jesting is applied in moderation, is not at anyone's expense and is based on truth, it is positive and beneficial, elevating rather than demeaning.

Generally jesting is a cause of illness and can lead to loss of respect, loss of reliability and certainty. People who joke too often lose the respect of others. With excessive laughter and jesting, their behaviour becomes unpredictable and unreliable. We often cannot rely or depend upon such people. It is for this reason that jesting is an illness of the self.

The cure for jesting is simply by not doing it. Question your motive and consider the probable effect before you decide to jest.

(f) Arrogance. Arrogance is closely related to conceit and pride. The difference is that the conceited person lies to himself, while the arrogant and proud person lies to others. The foundation of arrogance is ultimately lack of inner stability and contentment.

Arrogance manifests itself in a number of ways: in physical beauty, intelligence, in one's opinions, ideas, beliefs, ancestry, wealth, property, social status, reputation, and in the collective strength of one's country, community or society.

The reason that this illness is so critical is that on many levels it does not allow for any progress or cure for the self. For example, even if one is doing good, by having seen that one is doing good, that itself prevents one from benefiting from the liberation and freedom that come from good actions.

The cure for arrogance is to look beyond the cause of our arrogance. If it is good works, then the cure is to look beyond the self to the source of all goodness, the Merciful Creator.

Ultimately, the cure for all forms of arrogance is to pull its roots out from the heart, completely, by self-knowledge, watchfulness and awareness.

A practical treatment is to put oneself in a lower position than another. Whatever the form of arrogance may be – for example, pride in one's spiritual knowledge – one must recognise that there are others with greater knowledge than oneself. One should also keep company with those of greater gifts than oneself.

To overcome arrogance, one must practise putting oneself behind others and placing others before oneself, and also lowering oneself before one's elders. Practising humility by certain acts which we consider to be beneath ourselves, such as carrying luggage for others, taking food to the poor, watching one's manner of dress, so that we do not place ourselves above others by what we wear, and sometimes purposely wearing something that is ordinary and plain, and other similar acts of humility will help to bring about a cure.

It is always wise to see oneself as being smaller and less than other people at all times, and to practise humility. By constantly acknowledging our mistakes and what goes on within ourselves and publicly exposing it, the roots of arrogance will dry up and wither away.

(g) Scorn. Scorn is related to arrogance, its purpose being to lower another person's esteem, whether it be by harshness of language, tacit indication, or mockery. Its effect is to destroy, demean, belittle or lower the importance of another, thereby increasing one's own sense of self-worth. By showing disdain for others, one is at the same time asserting one's own self-importance, as well as minimising the possible threat of being unmasked or exposed.

The cure for scorn will come about eventually by the gradual breakdown of the cause of it. A basic method of treatment is to remind oneself constantly that one can be wrong, or that other viewpoints could be more correct than one's own. The outer behaviour of treatment for scorn is to listen rather than speak, to be patient, to restrain from pushing forward one's own opinion, and simply to refrain from belittling others. By conscientiously applying this method, a gradual change in one's attitude and behaviour will occur.

(h) Treachery. In whatever situation treachery occurs, it is expressed as disloyalty and betrayal. This is because treachery is a manifestation of a break in what was formerly a connected and unified situation. Treachery can be the result of a multitude of motives: unfounded suspicion, lack of gratitude – biting the hand that feeds us – not being valued and acknowledged as one feels one should be, and so on. Treachery, as in all illnesses of the self, is based on ignorance and injustice. Treachery is injustice to oneself and to others.

The way to treat this illness is to recognise the ignorance. For example, if treachery is the result of being misguided by anger, then one should not act when one is angry. One must stop when anger arises. Again, the most radical remedy is to face the cause of treachery within oneself and expose it to oneself and to others, whereby it will disappear like a thief when confronted. All of these illnesses disappear when faced, and the more often one confronts them at source, the faster they will disappear.

(i) Unfairness. Unfairness concerns imposing the burden of injustice on another by any number of ways. Unfairness is based on our material and animal limitations, such as anxiety and other related tendencies. Once any of our lower traits are allowed to guide our actions, unfairness is bound to arise.

Selfishness is a general description of a trait that brings about a great deal of unfairness. The selfish person will constantly justify hoarding, or cheating others out of their fair share, and so on.

If one is carried away by anger, then one will bring about a punishment that is unjust and far out of line, and incompatible with the cause itself.

The cure is to nip these lower traits in the bud before they grow. The most radical treatment is to consider oneself unfair at all times. However one judges others, if one judges oneself first and considers oneself as being unfair and unjust, then one will gradually begin to withdraw towards a more balanced and neutral position from which to act.

(j) Acquisitiveness. Here we find that virtually all humanity shares in the search for a measure of security in the form of material wealth, be they possessions, precious gems or other rare or desired objects. The fear of their loss, conversely, is a source of great insecurity, anxiety and stress.

There is a traditional story of a king whose subject brought him a most precious and unique crystal ball. This gift gave the king great happiness. It was kept in the safest place possible and he always derived the greatest pleasure and pride from exhibiting it. Until one day, the natural and inevitable thing happened to the crystal ball – its destruction. The king's grief was so great that he lost control over himself and thereby lost his kingdom. Thus an object that was meant to give joy and happiness ended up by being the source of the almost total destruction and ruin of the person concerned.

We know very well how much the possession of even ordinary belongings can cause grief and sorrow.

The belief that material possessions or precious objects are, quite rationally, considered to be useful security in times of calamity is often not at all the case. When the time comes for these objects to be liquidated, auctioned or sold, their owners often find they have overvalued them in their own eyes, or, perversely, that the merchants and middlemen now cause them to be undervalued. Far from being a means of alleviating the suffering of their owners, they cause greater grief. Even though objects are never safe from depreciation or loss, nevertheless, in times of insecurity and upheaval, one will always find people putting their own lives in danger for the sake of their possessions.

The root of this problem is the false notion of security in accumulation. Much energy and effort is spent in outer acquisitiveness and enrichment and not enough on true living or awareness, which is the only secure base. This recognition is the cure. Wealth may alleviate some material suffering, and although most of our suffering is non-material, its root cause is a lack of connection with the creational source and purpose. The ultimate cure, then, is to experience that life's purpose is to discover the meaning and nature of its source rather than to adore and accumulate its glitter and attributes in the world. In poverty or in wealth, in sickness or health, that source of life permeates all and is available to those who can see.

We have now covered the ten major causes of anger, which is the first of the major conditions of the power of repulsion.

The cure for anger is twofold – first by knowledge, and second by action. Knowledge is that the person should understand that what one is angry about is an event of reality, and that by anger itself, one will not achieve anything except hurting oneself. As for action, the angry person needs to take steps that will increase his awareness of his state of anger and thereby reduce the agitation. A very practical cure for anger is that if one is standing whilst in a state of anger, then one should sit, and if one is sitting, then one should lie down. Another very practical remedy when one is angry is to take oneself aside and wash one's face and one's hands with cold water or to perform the ritual ablution of *wudu*. To keep silent is yet another way of overcoming anger.

In states of calmness or meditation, one could reflect and remind oneself of the foolish and dangerous consequences of uncontrolled anger. Then, when one is in danger of giving way to anger, one can call up these images as an aid to controlling oneself, thereby gradually overcoming the condition of anger in oneself.

Further comments on anger are made by Rhazes.[4] He says that anger is put into an animal so that it may take revenge on another which causes it pain. However, when anger occurs in excess there is such a loss of control (of reason, in the case of humans) that the angry person often causes more harm to himself than to the object of its anger. It is known that anger and rage can bring on blindness in people. Rhazes remarks that there is no difference between a man in the extreme of rage and an actual lunatic or animal, for he has lost his reasoning and intellect.

Whilst anger is not fully eradicated in oneself, what one can do is to propel it in a positive direction. One can divert it towards the injustices and wrongs in this world until such time as one's anger becomes purely an instrument of justice and redressing the imbalances. Anger in this case can help to propel us forward towards the right path.

The ultimate cure for the condition of anger, according to Rhazes, is the recognition and application of justice. For anger is essentially a transgression and deviation from the path of justice and unity towards tyranny – a departure from equilibrium towards the direction of excess. Anyone who observes the proper conditions for justice and makes this one's habit will find the treatment of anger an easy matter.

Cowardice

The second condition of the power of repulsion is cowardice which arises out of neglect, and manifests itself as a lack of self-regard, general weakness in one's nature and faint-heartedness.

Cowardice implies that the heart is not supple or free, and is constricted.

The understanding of any virtue necessitates the understanding of its opposite. Anger is an emotion of the self brought about by an appetite for vengeance, whereas cowardice is a quietening or stilling of the self through vitiation of the appetite of vengeance.

A consequence of faint-heartedness is that the person abases himself and as a result becomes ill. Wrong desires will then begin to arise from this condition. When a heart has reached that condition, the situation will produce all sorts of side-effects, such as idleness, excess desire for comfort, love of luxury, and ease and the general result is a calamity in every way in one's existence and affairs.

As with any other disease, treatment depends on removing the cause. Removing the cause of cowardice involves bringing out the irascible motives in a proper way – that is, by making a person sufficiently angry about his own state and weaknesses so that he will wish to change, using the poison itself as the starting remedy. Where there is a sickness, therein lies its cure.

Certain masters have used the remedy of deliberately subjecting themselves and their followers to situations where dangers were faced, or embarking upon perilous journeys. They placed themselves in situations which brought about a natural confrontation with their own fears and cowardice – as a result, they set in motion a course of events that brought out their irascibility, of which courage is the ultimate virtue. Subjecting a person to these conditions in a properly guided manner can awaken and cause to grow in one that appropriate energy of anger, which is now used in a predetermined channel for a positive and balanced outcome.

Fear

The third condition of the power of repulsion is fear which arises out of perversion. Fear arises from the apprehension of something dangerous, undesirable or unpleasant; the expectation of something dreaded which, however, the person is incapable of repelling. Such apprehension and expectation may relate to a potential occurrence which does not yet actually exist. Whether these fears and apprehensions are the result of one's own actions or of circumstances outside one's control, the intelligent person will realise that unless something is done about the situation, those anxieties will in fact only hasten the occurrence of the feared outcome of that anxiety.

We have often experienced that yielding uncontrollably to fear can only result in hastening the very suffering that is feared before it even happens – we ourselves invoke the dreaded outcome.

If, however, one recognises that the repulsion of this occurrence is actually beyond the bounds of human capacity to deal with – and that this event is certainly going to come, is unavoidable, is already under way (for example, a year of bad harvest) – if one knows that the event is truly outside one's power to deal with, this realisation will help one to face and deal with the event or calamity in a state of much greater rationality, equilibrium and strength, thereby achieving effectiveness and success.

On the other hand, if one simply lapses into melancholy or inertia because of fear and dread, then one is deprived of even that amount of rational energy which one could muster in facing the inevitable. The person who has gained this much insight and wisdom will find comfort, calm and reliability in oneself.

All fear is ultimately based on ignorance. The person who is awakened, and whose intellect and higher faculties are in command over one's self and one's physical body, will be able to overcome events as and when they occur, without having been weakened previously by anxieties and fear.

Fear of Death

The fear of death is one of the hardest fears to overcome; and since it is also one of the most common (as well as the most severe), we shall comment upon it in some detail.

Fear of death occurs mainly because we do not know the nature of death since we have not experienced that event yet. We usually suppose that the decay and breakdown of the physical body is the final end of the whole affair for us – and yet the world, with whatever attachments we have had to it, still carries on.

Some fear death because they think it is accompanied by great pain, more severe even than the pain of disease that may lead to death. Others fear death because of the punishment they believe will come after. Others are simply perplexed and full of doubt about the aftermath. Others fear death mainly because of their various regrets over what they did or did not do during their lives. All of these fears are due to our ignorance regarding the nature of the final journey of the self, and its condition after separation from the body.

The majority of people's fears are groundless, because the source of fear is mainly due to ignorance.

Death may be defined as the self's non-employment of the bodily organs, and when the self has attained what it was created for, the body as a physical vehicle has served its purpose. (Death can also occur, of course, regardless of whether a person has had the full opportunity to reach his highest potential and attain awakening.)

The self, however, is regarded as an enduring substance which does not disappear with the annihilation of the body, and thereby brings about one's main fear of death because one does not know where the ultimate abode of one's immortal soul is. Fear of death is thus due to ignorance and not to death itself. The anxiety to avoid death is due to ignorance of its nature and reality.

Treatment of the Fear of Death

There is no other treatment for ignorance except knowledge. One only needs to be awakened so that one can put one's fears towards a positive outcome. In the situation of the person who does not know what will be the state of his soul after death, the remedy lies in first admitting ignorance. Then, as one learns more about the nature and meaning of life experientially and about the hereafter from the prophetically revealed knowledges, confidence, certainty and knowledge will grow and fear will vanish.

Wise men throughout the ages have contented themselves with the necessary modicum of needs, detaching their heart from excesses, luxuries and the superficialities of life, and putting an end (or 'being dead') to their desires. That is why death is said to be of two types, voluntary and natural. Life also is of two types, voluntary and natural.

By voluntary death is meant death of the appetites and desires, and freedom from those difficulties that arise from desire. This is a wilful, voluntary act and a most praiseworthy discipline and cure. Natural death is the natural departure of the soul from the body.

Voluntary life refers to the transient and worldly life, contingent on eating, drinking and so on; whereas real natural life is everlasting, permanent in gladness and joy. One would think the reverse would be the case but it is not.

This is why we naturally long for everlasting life and naturally desire longevity. It is in our nature to want permanency and dependability, and this desired situation is called natural life. Voluntary life however is that of departure – because in fact there is a certain measure of will associated with that departure.

As far as the individual is concerned, one has a measure of free will as to when to leave this world and to cease experiencing life in this physical reality. The extent to which one cares for the body certainly affects the duration of one's life.

It is really an unfortunate person whose soul, prior to leaving its body, is still inclined towards corporeal and physical pleasures, fearing to leave them. Such a person is farthest away from truth. Certainly he is on his way to a more painful abode than the one he is in. Such persons have not understood the Prophetic tradition, 'Die before you die' (referring to the death of desires and appetites), and have not reached their full potential of enlightenment.

For the person who is fearful of death on the presumption that the next abode is necessarily painful, the treatment is to recognise the falsehood of that presumption. To prove how false is this presumption we notice that whenever the body is not affected by the soul – when, for example, it is in deep sleep – it has no sensation of pain. So the existence of pain occurs only because of the intermediary existence and awareness of the self.

It is thus evident that death is a state whose existence is not related to any sensation on the part of the body. Physical sensation is to do entirely with the presence of the self in the body. At death, that which caused the comprehension of pain in the body (the soul, or self) has already departed. So how can the body then feel pain?

Fear of Punishment after Death

As for those who fear the punishment that comes after death, punishment can only be executed upon something that endures. This person is therefore acknowledging the continuation of some part of oneself after death, while at the same time confessing to the transgressions and errors for which punishment is merited. This being so, his fears really concern his own errors and transgressions, not death as such. So fear in its essence is a deterrent, and a useful one in that it should make one stop committing these wrong deeds and transgressions and return once again to balance, equilibrium and justice (towards oneself and creation at large).

It is strange that what is feared here (punishment after death) does not always have the effect of making a person abandon his erroneous ways. That which could have an effect – awareness of one's behaviour causing one to take to the path of virtue – is ignored.

So we conclude that death does not mean what the common people suppose. What is generally meant by fear of death is a consequence of ignorance (and a force to propel us towards discovery and knowledge).

Take the case of the one who is aware of the inevitability and necessity of death and yet aspires to long life. This person should be reminded that whoever desires long life is in fact desiring old age, and old age is accompanied by many obvious personal, physical limitations and undesirable side-effects. With old age one also experiences other unpleasant events, such as the death of loved ones and friends. So what is longed for (in long life) is ultimately undesirable misfortune!

But when we attain the certainty that death means only that our essence, our real self or soul, departs from the metaphorical or the figurative body, so to speak, which has been put together from the four fundamental creations (earth, water, air and fire) and then placed in the service of the soul or self for its numbered days in this existence, in order to enable a perfection of the soul to escape from this impediment of a body and detach itself from its excesses and corruption, then we have acquired the true meaning of death. By reflecting on this certainty one realises that the self actually gains enormously – not loses – by departing from this world.

So when we awaken to the reality of the self and the nature of the hereafter, we realise the transitory nature of the physical body. Thus whenever the opportunity arises for such awakened beings to give up this body in the cause of reality, truth or justice, they are prepared and unafraid – willing and happy – to do so.

Plato says many regard death as a great affliction and hate it, but if they reflected upon the affair of death, they would consider it a great blessing and something to look forward to. They would regard it as a great goodness, for death is a completion of our nature; man's real description is he who is living, speaking and who will die, for man indeed – even though he may remain in ignorance of it – is destined for the next life.

Further Treatment of the Fear of Death

Advice on the treatment of the fear of death is offered by the theologian Rhazes. He points out that this fear can only be entirely and permanently banished by the knowledge that one is passing to a better state than this. We must, therefore, acquire such knowledge.

The person who is afraid of death actually dies a thousand times in the course of his life. He is always thinking of it. Yet since death is inevitable for everyone, it is quite useless to dwell upon the fact of it.

There are really only two positions, argues Rhazes. One is that death is the end of everything, in which case there can be no consequences of any kind arising out of it, so no cause for fear. The second and proper position, however, is to realise that not only is death not the end, but that it is entirely within our power to make sure that our next life will be happier than this one. All we need to do is to act correctly, and submit to and follow the divinely revealed laws. If we only do this, then death, far from being any matter to be feared, will be no less than our passport to eternal bliss.

Nor in this connection, concludes Rhazes, need we worry that we will be insufficiently righteous, for God only asks that we try our best. He does not ask us or expect us to achieve beyond our capacity. Therefore doing our best to our capacity is enough.

In summary, then, fear of death is based on ignorance, and there is no real treatment for ignorance except knowledge. One only needs to be awakened so that one can put one's fears toward a positive outcome. As one learns more about the nature and meaning of life experientially, and about the afterlife from the prophetically revealed knowledges, confidence, certainty and knowledge will grow and fear will vanish. So the fear or remembrance of death itself becomes the greatest remedy.

Conditions of the Faculty of Discrimination

In considering the discriminative faculty, Tusi points out the following as the most severe of its conditions: (1) perplexity, which arises out of excess; (2) simple ignorance, which arises out of neglect; and (3) compounded ignorance, which arises out of perversion.

1. *Perplexity*. The source of this condition is excess, and it is related to being troubled by guile, cleverness or excessive ingenuity.

Perplexity and confusion generally arise from contradictory arguments, facts involving difficult questions, and the inability of the person involved to ascertain the truth. The way to treat this situation is to acquire the habit of reflection on the basic premises of the opposing arguments. One must make a decisive judgement as to the invalidity of one or more of the basic contradictory points. One must make up one's mind as an act of will.

One must adhere to rational logic in scrutinising the premises of the problem that one is investigating. By doing so, one may discover error or fault in the basic premises that have caused perplexity.

2. *Simple ignorance*. The source of this condition is neglect, which manifests itself as an inadequacy in one's ability to speculate or discern, or as stupidity or foolishness.

Ignorance is initially not blameworthy, for its existence is obviously a precondition of learning. Moreover the very genesis of the human species occurs in this state of ignorance. It becomes blameworthy, however, to remain in ignorance and not to progress along the road of learning. In fact, ignorance itself propels the person naturally towards knowledge and the comfort that arises when ignorance is dispelled.

Ignorant behaviour will usually result in regret, because the person concerned had not intended to cause himself or others any harm. If he remains ignorant, he will repeatedly go off course and end up in disappointment and sorrow.

Treatment here depends much on reflection, meditation and awareness. Upon such reflection one becomes aware of the superior gifts of the human being over other inmates of this planet because of his ability to discriminate and reason – to learn.

3. *Compounded ignorance*. The source of this condition is perversion, which manifests itself as a yearning for knowledge which does not assist in the development of the self,

seeking instead essentially irrelevant information and facts that are not conducive or helpful towards one's growth and self-perfection.

The nature of this particular form of ignorance is not that the self is devoid of any knowledge, but that it is preoccupied with facts, information and forms of invalid conviction. The problem is the false certainty that one in fact does know. No vice is more destructive than the vice of clinging to false knowledge.

Just as physicians of the body are incapable of treating certain diseases or chronic conditions, so too do the physicians of the soul often find themselves incapable of treating this particular condition of the psyche. For despite the distorted forms of knowledge to which the self is attached, there is no awareness of what is wrong, and where there is no awareness there can be no desire for amelioration.

One possible approach to remedy this condition is to set the patient to acquire some of the skills of formal reasoning and logic, such as are found within the mathematical, natural and physical sciences, so that one can become aware of the pleasure of certainty and the perfection and beauty of truth. This could be a door to the realisation of one's arrogance and over-confidence, thereby prompting a step in the direction towards recovery.

Concerning knowledge, Ali ibn Abi Talib says that there are four types of people. There are those who know, and who know that they know: they are enlightened ones so follow them. Then there are those who know, but who do not know that they know: these are people of knowledge who are unaware of their station, so remind them that they know. Then there are the people who do not know, and who know that they do not know. This category covers most people in this existence, and among them are the seekers of knowledge and the followers of truth who desire to achieve the most fully virtuous lives in this world and the next. Help these people. Then there are those who do not know, but who are unaware that they do not know. These are people for whom there is very little hope, and their company is to be avoided.

Nowadays, however, we find a fifth predominating category of people and they are the ones who do not know but claim knowledge. What is to be done with them?

Other Conditions of the Self

We now turn to a number of other common conditions of the self.

Grief

Grief is defined by Tusi as the result of many possible causes – the loss of loved ones, the failure to obtain a desired object, and so on. Generally, all causes are associated with a failure to satisfy a corporeal demand or appetite, allied with the regret that comes with that loss or failure.

Upon reflection, we conclude that it is impossible for us at all times to satisfy all our appetitive or repulsive desires. That could be only partially possible if we were absolute monarchs or possessed divine powers. So the fewer desires of attraction or repulsion that we have, the more likely it is that we will not be grieved or disappointed. One should therefore content oneself with the minimum amount necessary to fulfil only basic needs and to meet one's urgent necessities, considering these as obligatory. One will avoid accumulation and the desire for multitudes of possessions. By this, one will attain benefit without dread and be joyful, with minimum distress or grief.

Now, we ask, why is it that all affairs in this world have in them an element of grief? Even in the most joyful or pleasurable occasions lies an element of grief. Is it because of the fact that these occasions will come to an end?

Grief is nature's way of telling us, its children, that outer pleasures are only meant to remind us that what we really desire is a state of homeostasis based on equilibrium, peace and contentment, and that the door to such joy lies ultimately within us. The causes of pleasures and their circumstances are themselves not going to last – and the fact of this transiency may be at the root of our grief. The state of joy – complete contentment without agitation or imbalance – is a reflection of our basic original nature and possible end in bliss and joy.

The rational attitude is to be content with what is possible and available, while not lamenting or regretting what has been lost or that which is beyond one's reach.

The Nature of Grief

Most of us have encountered people who have suffered

great emotional or material disasters through loss of family, children, homes and other possessions. But after a lapse of time, they seem to regain a calm, steady or happy state and seem to overcome those losses entirely.

This observation proves once again that grief is not directly related to the event itself – the object of loss after all is still lost. So is grief not permanent because it is of a different reality?

Ali ibn Abi Talib's advice is to show fortitude, as befits the noble-minded, or to seek forgetfulness, as do the beasts. Either way one will overcome grief; with fortitude however, virtue grows.

Thus in no sense does conventional suffering or unhappiness find acceptance with the one who has attained awakening. If we allow ourselves to be overcome by grief for the passing of everything lost, we must then always be grieving. Why should the intelligent person constantly expend his life on matters that would both harm him and give him pain? After all, beasts of burden do not grieve.

Treatment of Grief

A general remedy for grief is to reflect upon other people's lives and the variety of their desires, objectives and modes of existence. One will learn the truth of what has been already analysed above as being applicable also in one's own life. One can only conclude that those people must be utterly irrational who, heedless of the nature of reality and the meaning of happiness, constantly pursue the gratification of desires that can in fact never be satisfied.

Those who constantly run after transitory gratifications, which only add more fuel to the fire of wanting, are contrasted with those who recognise the delights and the joys of inner awakening and the growth of their enlightenment and awareness. One pursuit is only too transient and has no lasting benefit; the other is permanent. No one can detract from another what one has acquired in one's intellect and heart, whereas all other acquisitions can be lost.

Further Comments on Grief

The philosopher Al-Kindi describes grief as a state that people attract to themselves by their own wrong choices, and that it is not connected with natural objects – that is, grief has nothing to do with natural, physical, external or other realities, but we bring it upon ourselves.

A house may collapse, for example, and the owner will grieve, whereas this event may not affect you or me. The natural occurrence or event brings grief to the owner because of his relationship and attachment to it, whereas others who had no relationship with the house are not affected by the event.

Let the person who has lost anything that he desired, or who has been disappointed in failing to achieve a desire or objective, reflect with the detached eye of wisdom on the cause of his grief. Or let that same person also take the example of one who has suffered loss, but then has come to accept that deprivation and is now content. It then becomes clear, concludes Al-Kindi, that grief is neither necessary nor inevitable.

Rhazes points out that since grief, like anger, clouds both thought and reason, it is sensible from every point of view to try to banish it. This can be done in two ways – firstly, by avoiding in advance occasions which we realise are going to cause grief; and secondly, by dealing with grief at once, should an occasion for it arise. Look into the nature of grief, examine it, ascertain its cause and try to analyse and understand it; but above all, do not taste, savour or embrace the grief, or be in any way reluctant to part with it.

One of the most common causes of sorrow is the loss of loved ones. Therefore it is wise to temper the degree of this kind of emotional love which we create. It is wise to remember that this person or that child is only on loan to us. It is in the nature of things that he or she will one day leave or pass away. Fanning the flames of attachment and love to great heat will in no way at all alter the inevitable outcome and fact of life. On the contrary, it will make the outcome far worse when it occurs.

As in other cases of dealing with the conditions of the self, Rhazes counsels us to picture and imagine the loss of the loved one before it actually happens. Say to oneself, 'He or she is now gone, and I am alone without him or her'. Just as athletes train for a race, to strengthen themselves before the event, we should train for the moment of loss. To do the opposite, to shut out all thought of losing the loved one, is only to store up greater future shock and grief.

Rhazes also counsels that we should have many people whom we love equally, not one or two special people. That way it will be easier to bear the loss of any specific one of our companions. The prudent farmer plants many kinds of crops, not placing all his trust in the success of one crop only.

Also, think not of the outrage that occurs when some loved thing or person is taken away. Instead be grateful that one has had the blessing and comfort of it at least for a while. Remember, too, that misfortune and unhappiness also pass away.

In summary, intelligent and wise living are our best remedies against grief. Wise men in all ages have always offered similar counsel. When Socrates, for example, was asked why he was always cheerful and never grieving, he replied, 'It is because I set my heart on nothing that would leave me griefstricken if lost'.

Sadness

One of the major causes of sadness (as distinct from grief or misery) is greed, in the sense of excessive, unrealistic desire and expectations. The constant remembrance of lost opportunities and of what might have been are the causes of sadness.

A general cure is constantly and forcefully to remind oneself that everything in this world is subject to decay and disappearance. Even if we achieve whatever is our heart's desire (fame, riches, power), that contentment itself would not last. Whatever is constant in this world is only in the realm of comprehension, intellect and inner knowledge acquired by awakening to reality. If one concentrates on that which endures, then one can move gradually out of the condition of sadness.

Misery and Sorrow

Misery and sorrow do not occur to the animal self nor to the simplistic person. For example, simplistic people and innocent young children do not feel deep or lasting tragic emotion. For them, unhappiness is of a much less deep and more fleeting nature. For them also, the same is true of happiness; both sorrow and happiness come about rapidly and depart quickly.

Misery and despondency are of two types. One type belongs to people who are veiled (i.e. engrossed in this world and its darkness). The second belongs to the hypocrites. They were originally able to accept the light of knowledge through innate development, but they deviated from the way with the result that their path has become narrowed, their hearts sealed and their baser tendencies more pronounced. They dwell in their lower nature, seeking to satisfy every desire. Although they once glimpsed the light of freedom, they now remain tossed by the vicissitudes of life, suffering from duality and its confusion.

Treatment of Misery and Sorrow

There are two types of misery and sorrow, and one is virtually a chronic and incurable condition. This type afflicts those who are completely entrenched in devious ways, and who as a result do not evolve. Spiritual teachers cannot help such people, for they are childish and feeble in their intellect. They are the people of the world, and of lower tendencies.

The second type of misery and sorrow has to do with the intellect, and this type can be cured. This is the type of person who once was able to accept the light of knowledge before deviating from the path.

Conditions of the Heart

One of the Prophetic traditions relates that there is in the human being an organ and if it is sound, the body will be sound; if it is sick, the entire body will be ill – this organ is the heart.

Generally speaking, the conditions of the heart are considered to be connected with ignorance, uncertainties, doubts and other similar disturbed states that will cloud its clarity and direction. As a result, its unific connectedness is weakened and undermined. The condition of the heart, therefore, comes when there is a mixture of faith and denial of the truth, of trust in the one encompassing reality and doubt. When a person's heart is in this disturbed state, what emanates from him are confusing and contradictory intentions and actions. The end result for that person is ever-greater insecurity, disconnectedness, confusion and suffering.

This condition of the heart is different from the sickness that afflicts people of hypocrisy, for it is caused by the weakness of faith, knowledge and experience, whereas a hypocrite is one whose tongue professes a state whilst his heart is not in fact in that state. Hypocrisy, therefore, is not a condition of the heart as such, but a disconnectedness of the heart.

Treatment of the Conditions of the Heart

We are given indications of cures for the heart in the Qur'an:

> To Him [Reality] ascend the good words, and the good deeds elevate them.(35:10)

The Prophet said, 'The good deed wipes out the wrong deed'. So the treatment can be brought about when we move on to better and nobler deeds, overcoming and leaving behind the old, selfish deeds. If one who is ill at heart wants to be cured, he has to turn to Reality in repentance and regret, and trust that he will come to understand, experience and know the truth.

The person who is ill at heart must also attend constantly to the improvement of his intentions, and to back up those intentions with continual better actions. Otherwise, such people will be as described in the Qur'an:

> Do they not see that they are tried once or twice in every year yet they do not turn [to Reality] nor do they take heed. (9:126)

To turn to reality is to remember all – appropriate outer actions backed by pure intentions.

Others hold the view that the condition of the heart itself will lead to its own cure. When the self opposes its desires, then its illness will become its cure.

According to another view,[5] practical advice is prescribed to treat the condition of hardness of heart. To begin with, one should fast. If after continued fasting one still finds that one's heart has not turned and softened, then one should increase one's prayers. If one's state still continues after that, one should make sure that one is not committing any act that is disagreeable or forbidden. If the condition remains, one must undertake to serve one's relations and friends and connect with them. If further remedy is needed, one must extend that kindness and service to orphans and other needy members of one's community. It is by extending oneself and giving to others that breaks the barriers of the selfish and encased heart. When love flows in action with no expectations, we know the heart is in a sound state.

Safeguarding the Health of the Self

The health and healing of the self, according to Tusi, is equated with the acquisition and retention of the appropriate virtues. He says that nothing has greater effect on the self or soul than a companion or close friend. For this reason, one must be on guard against the intimacy and fellowship of persons not adorned with noble talents, and especially against the interaction with those of immoral or defective character.

Another philosopher, Al-Kindi, says that the seeker after virtue should take advantage of the state of others' behaviour which leads to bad actions, in order to censure oneself with the reproach of each act as if the action had actually proceeded from oneself rather than from others, thereby benefiting from them. Moreover, at the end of each day, one should carry out an examination of every action of one's own performed during that day.

Al-Kindi also says we should not be content, like a passive treatise or book, to instruct others in wisdom whilst we ourselves remain without it, or be like a whetstone, which sharpens iron but is unable to cut. Rather, we should be like the sun diffusing light from our essence upon the moon of the self, so as to lend its likeness to it. This is precisely the desirable state as regards the diffusion of virtue.

We can preserve the health of the self by following a sane and balanced way of life which can best be achieved by adherence to a divinely revealed code of conduct. This adherence on the inner level would bring the recognition of the higher powers and forces within the self, thereby enhancing the virtuous values within oneself.

As far as the world is concerned, the more worldly goods one employs to fill one's wants, the greater is one's true poverty, because the greater is one's dependency on transient, material objects. The less dependent we are on worldly possessions, the greater can be our inner strength and wealth.

The wisdom is to acquire habits of restraint and self-control, especially in respect of the gratification of appetites or whenever one is assailed by one of the lower elements, such as anger. If one can achieve these goals, then virtue follows as a matter of course.

Those who thus contain and restrain themselves, even though surrounded by fools, become shielded from folly, abuse and neglectfulness. These enlightened individuals are able to tolerate the presence of all kinds of evil and not be affected by them. The wayward life of others cannot influence or deflect them.

In summary, then, those who seek a means of preserving the health of the self, as we have mentioned before, must not pursue this quest in isolation. The knowledge and availability of a specialist are conducive to a rapid cure. The loving guidance of expert knowledge is indispensable. Apart from monitoring progress, the knowledgeable and awakened guide will skilfully encourage the seeker towards the ultimate freedom, by recognition of the limitations of enslavement – towards the highest form of freedom within and the perfection of the limiting factors of physical reality.

Once full understanding and experience of the symptoms and conditions of the self have been discovered, and remedies and cures have been practised and applied, the individual can attain the wisdom of self-reflection and rehabilitation. The process of the awareness of the symptoms and the administering of the remedy can be developed by the individual to such an extent that the two aspects of the process become almost instantaneous, without much of a time lapse. The dynamics of self-knowledge are now at work and its time-loop is ever shrinking.

For example, when anger is aroused, an inner aspect of the individual instantly captures that state and signals the remedy. Such an evolved seeker can be said to have begun the mastery of one's self by the self. Where there is an ailment, there is also the cure, all too spontaneously – unitive in origin and uniting in symptom and cure.

This instant cure, rebalance and centralisation of the being is the right ecology for self-fulfilment to set in. As we have said, every individual has within him the goal of self-fulfilment and the capacity for clear reflection, but it begins to be experienced only once the impurities of the heart are removed and held at bay.

This stage of maturity enables the seeker to start the process of higher unfoldment and transcendence. Up to this point we can call the processes of the seeker's healing both subjective and objective. From now on, it will be primarily subjective and experiential. Once the cybernetics of self-healing and self-awareness sets in properly, we are into the realm of self-knowledge and glorious self-unfoldment. This is the ambience of real self-fulfilment.

Conclusion

In this chapter, we have examined the most prevalent conditions of the self, and have proposed various remedies and cures for them. In conclusion, we could add here that there are five steps of remembrance in the remedy of any of the self's conditions.

The first is to remember the origin of the condition (e.g. greed, desiring to own the world – which is impossible to attain).

The second is to remember the maintaining of it (which is a difficulty and a burden, and ultimately, impossible – for death will come).

The third is to remember the Creator, Allah.

The fourth is to remember that this condition is a barrier to further evolvement and elevation.

Finally, the fifth is to remember that there is no reality behind the condition itself.

In the final chapter, we will illustrate by examples how the self is already hallmarked by the unific stamp. We shall see how the self throughout its life manifests characteristics and tendencies towards its unific origin, and how, at all times, it is connected to the unific factor underlying it. All has emanated from One, by the grace of One, sustained by One and returning to One. The imagination of multiplicity in this world is part of the love and return back to the same One.

5

The Unified Self

Through a random sampling of episodes and patterns of behaviour from real life, we shall illustrate in this final chapter how our experiences, behaviour and attitudes are already hallmarked by the unific stamp. We are bondsmen who have been ingrained by the one and only Reality which we come to discover and know through its attributes and actions, and whose oneness was before creation and is the same now, who is beyond time and has created time, so that its attribute of eternal unity could be understood as being the opposite shore from where we now stand in this passing world of experiential duality.

We have seen that this existence is based on a rhythmic, dynamic play which has no stability in itself, and is only a map that indicates the ever stable terrain of higher consciousness and unity. Like the Islamic teachings, the doctrines of Hinduism, as well as Taoism, are based on the idea that the multitudinous phenomena around us are but manifestations of the one ultimate reality. The Buddhists further declare that all things arise and pass away, and the idea of the separate individual is an illusion.

In this concluding chapter, we shall see how the self throughout its life manifests characteristics and tendencies towards its unific origin. The self at all times is connected to the unific factor underlying it. Hopefully by the variety of examples given, the reader will be able to see for himself endless other experiences and observations from his or her own life that illustrate the unified self. It is hoped that the reader will add to our sampling, which is indeed one of the goals of this work.

The following examples are grouped according to a natural progression of the self's journey in this life. Beginning at Birth and Early Growth, through a lifetime of Learning, Experiencing and Awareness, until its final Awakening and Spiritual Maturity, we see a variety of examples to illustrate the unific tendency of the self.

Birth and Early Growth

These examples show how the self's unific tendency begins to assert itself from the moment of birth and its earliest years of life.

The Star at the Centre

The point of emergence and the beginning of human life resembles the birth of a star. For both the human being and the star, it all begins with the act of physical birth. The same way that the star is interlinked and relates to the infinite cosmos, the human consciousness interlinks with its environment and to time and space before and after its existence. At the same time, each being acts as though it is central to all that goes on around it and that every other creation peripheral to it. Most people, especially children, wish to be noticed and at the centre of attention. Each individual being thinks he is something special and seeks acknowledgement.

The key lies in the fact that each of us reflects the same aspect of the truth which lies within. The Qur'an says that man was not created frivolously. The heart of the human being contains the truth of the absolute uniqueness and central importance of the creational source. That truth is at the core of all creation, and because man inherently and potentially contains the secret of all creation, he sees himself at its centre.

We also see behind all childish behaviour, there is clearly and innocently a unifying factor. The motivation behind most behaviour is related to the nature of the source of creation. As we have seen earlier, most behaviour stems from the love of the all-powerful, all-present, all-loving, all-seeing, all-knowing, or any other of the attributes of reality. The child exhibiting his strength or playing with powerful toy engines is an echo of the almighty, all-powerful within. He is playing God or emperor! The childish boasts that 'My father is stronger than yours', or 'My mother is more beautiful than yours', are echoes that its origin is the greatest and the best, the highest source. The child calling out, 'Watch me!' 'Look at me!' is a reminder to see at all times only the reality that pervades all. Everyone must take notice!

Our love of order and routine – even though children appear to live in disorder and chaos – is a reflection of the divine attributes of reliability, stability and certainty. Generally, repetitive routine induces a certain stability and productivity. Fear of the dark is a reflection of our fear of the unknown and our love of light and knowledge by which we relate and unify. Our pleasure in giving gifts is an echo of the divine attribute of generosity within.

The perceptive eye will always see the unifying force of reality in every behavioural act, whether childish or adult. The reason we see it more clearly in the child's behaviour is that its actions are more single-pointed and less complex.

The Prophet enjoins us to remember that children look upon us as their lord, so we must behave in a manner that reflects the natural and revealed divine laws; otherwise, they will have great difficulty in discovering the true Lord later on in life.

Learning, Experiencing and Awareness

Most of life is spent in learning, experiencing and expanding in awareness. The examples given in this section are only a sampling of the variety of experiences we pass through. Throughout one's life, we experience continuous outer change, yet at the same time, we strive for inner stability and constancy, ever-unified with the non-changing reality.

Outer and Inner Power

From our earliest years, we all tend to express a love of and desire for power, a love of authority to dispense judgement and the subtler means of intellectual power. They all point to the inherent cause or centre of all power – the all-powerful that lies within.

One of the reasons we love power is because we desire to

direct our destiny in harmony towards fulfilment. Our love of power could bring us to the point of realising that through outer power and control we cannot attain our original objective, that of fulfilment at all times. We may then realise that the love of power and control was a reflection of the truth that the all-powerful is within us; and, once it is realised, we will no longer continue to exhibit the outer drive for power but simply acknowledge the 'power hologram' within. It is for this reason that we find the awakened ones are in true outer humility, yet they possess vast inner power, strength and certainty.

Biting the Hand that Feeds

Early in life we also begin to experience and acknowledge our dependence and interdependence on others. Even though we know there can be no absolute independence, either materially or emotionally, in this world, we nonetheless constantly seek it, driven by our insecurity if we become too dependent on a single individual or a limited source for our material or emotional sustenance.

For as soon as a reliable and dependable source is found, we either undermine it or look for other sources. We do this because we confuse the outer with the inner, the material with the spiritual. Whilst we need steady, reliable sources for our outer sustenance, for our inner, spiritual sustenance, we shall never rest until we awaken to the truth of the unific centre within. It is there that this independent, self-sustaining reality can be found. When we confuse our outer dependence with the inner, we commit the irrationality of biting the hand that feeds us, then wonder why!

The Qur'an reminds the Prophet that he is not the provider, keeper or controller of anyone. At best, he is a guide and a friend. Allah is the provider of all, the controller of all, and guides whoever is ready according to the extent of his ability.

Putting our Best Foot Forward

Why we generally like to appear to others at our best and do not want to be seen at our worst, whether physically, emotionally or otherwise, is because there is an inner drive to aspire to be better in every way. It is as though we want to help nature in its intended evolutionary purpose, as if we want to assist an ingrained natural programme within ourselves to bring out the best in us. It is a reflection that potentially we are the best.

All of this is an outer reflection of an inner reality within us which is the source of all that is best. Allah says in a Prophetic tradition, 'I am as good as your expectation of me'. So our experiences are the fruits of the seeds of our real intentions.

At the same time, there is a tendency in us not to want to see or hear anything disagreeable – an inbuilt mechanism that causes us to want to be shielded, or to disappear, from distressing scenes. We see this, for example, in the child who has done something wrong and buries its face in its hands or behind its mother's skirt, or in the faces of people who press the wrong elevator button, then wish that they could disappear when the doors open at the wrong floor!

Each of us can probably recount numerous occasions in our lives when we wished we could have vanished from the scene. The reason for this is that we dislike anything that is disturbing, discontinuous or disharmonious, for in truth, the laws of nature and the foundation of existence are based on harmony and unity, and we do not like to be a witness to their transgression. The unific reality within makes its presence felt and acknowledged by multitudes of outer behavioural acts!

Pleasing Others

We have all experienced wanting to please others, whether a child seeking approval, adults exchanging gifts or simply a human being hoping to give pleasure to another. The root of wanting to please is the desire to connect, and thus reduce the fears, insecurity, agitation or uncertainty that might exist in our relationships. One is pleased if one does something that is satisfying to another, because one has thereby relieved a desire or imbalance in that person and this kind of action announces that one is caring and ready to help.

Pleasing others is a reflection that we at all times want to bring harmony, equilibrium and contentment to others and to ourselves. We are universally ingrained to bring about well-being and unity. The divine source within the human heart always encourages us to give, share and care. Its unific and generous nature is reflected in us to varying

degrees, according to the extent of our turning and submission to it.

The Qur'an says that all humanity is created from one self.
One discovers that if we are truly good to ourselves, we are
likely to be good to others.

Dressing for the Occasion

Another means by which we attempt to unify is by the
way we dress. Our outer dress generally relates to the
climate and environment we find ourselves in, and also
reflects certain social, cultural and economic significance.
The businessman dresses in a fashion which reflects his
work and the degree of his seriousness or his concern about
the image of his business. On holiday the same businessman
dresses casually which is a reflection of his mood. It is quite
natural to dress for the occasion. We let our clothing communicate an aspect of our mood, intention or expectation,
thereby creating harmony by unifying our inner desire with
our outer achievement.

Our manner of dress, then, is in a small way yet another
instrument of unification. For those beings who have discovered the true meaning of inner harmony and contentment
and who are in a stable condition, they are always dressed
for the occasion.

The Prophet enjoins us to talk to people according to
their language and understanding. Our clothing is the outer
jacket of the book that lies within our breast. It is a means of
outer connection with others – for we are essentially unific
creatures.

Unitive Body

Another aspect of wholeness and unity is experienced by the
human body when it is in pain. The entire body is aware of the
disturbance, and attention is turned to it so that something
may be done to remove the cause of the agitation, thus
restoring equilibrium to the body. The body, then, has an
internal mechanism for bringing about peace, harmony and
tranquillity to all parts of the whole.

This drive towards unification and harmony can be seen in
every fragment of creation. The mechanism of equilibrium to
redress an imbalance or a disturbance that has been caused
by some interference is built into the creational system. Every

individual entity, human or other, seeks its optimum stability and equilibrium. The entire universe seems programmed to seek its proper balance. This balance is ultimately based on the balance and equilibrium between the multitudes of sub-systems and objects within them. So the macrocosmic state is based on the microcosmic. All systems seem caught in an attitude of unitive poise, but it is only the human being who has the consciousness of recognising the overall power of the unified and unifying Creator. It is humankind which can recognise that every separate body or system is caught in a unitive net cast out by the Merciful One.

Stilling the Mind

We all seek that state of peace and calm when the mind is momentarily at rest. We all want to be lifted from the distractions of the lower self and the limiting physical bonds of the body. It is for this reason that many seek out such means as taking to drink or drugs, to forget the problems and misery of the past and to reduce or drive away the fears and anxieties of the future. But the temporary relief from such a means – for example, alcohol – does not help to remove the cause that brought about the bondage in the first place. It is only a short-lived treatment of a symptom. What is really needed is to awaken oneself to the tyranny of the lower self and to break the bonds of attachment and fanciful desire.

The word 'alcohol' is derived from the Arabic word *al-kohl* which is the name of a balsam, a remedy for the eye, which also serves as a cosmetic to adorn the eye. Linguistically, therefore, *al-kohl* is that medicine which both strengthens the eye and renders clearer sight whilst it also beautifies the eye. In our present societies, alcohol is the temporary relief for stresses and anxieties, which nonetheless exacts a price upon the health and psyche.

Sight is only useful if it leads to insight. The ultimate insight is to see the constantly changing impermanency of physical reality and its constant, unchanging essence whose secret and product we are.

Physical and Spiritual Unification

We see in the experience of sexual union, the ultimate attempt to unite at a physical level. A point can be reached in the act when the mind is single-purposed and achieves a state of non-thought. The mind is then momentarily at rest. This state is a foretaste of the calm and contentment which we long for in this life, and which is a feature of higher consciousness.

We have seen that this world is based on duality and on opposites. Human consciousness is the interspace where the opposites meet. When the male and female meet in harmony, love and complementarity, the possibilities of subjectively experiencing inexplicable joy and contentment become real. This state comes about at the point when physical and mental awareness is minimal.

Similarly, the spiritual seeker practises meditation and conscious non-thought until he transcends awareness of the body. When all mental processes cease, a new state of pure consciousness can be experienced. At a higher stage, the experiencer and the experience merge, and an indescribable zone is entered. This state of pure bliss attained by the seeker is the spiritual equivalent of the physical pleasure shared by the man and woman in sexual love.

In all true systems of wisdom and spiritual teachings, we find that the opposites are regarded as two sides of the same reality, or extreme aspects of a single whole. Opposites are interdependent and in dynamic complementarity.

Inner Freedom and Outer Attachment

We become involved at all times in relationships which curtail some aspect of our freedom of choice. As we grow older, our physical and emotional life becomes more limited. The irony is that on the one hand we desire freedom and on the other we seek relationships which naturally limit our freedom. Indeed, as we progress in life our entanglements and limitations altogether increase – as a silkworm becomes more enclosed in its own cocoon. Yet at all times we seek greater freedom at all levels and in all spheres. How can this conflict be overcome?

This situation can be resolved only by an increase of inner freedom, the freedom which comes as a result of knowledge of the unific reality, whilst one continues to be involved and bound outwardly.

As we progress in this life, nature presents us with ever-increasing outer limitations. The narrowing of our personal habits and physical activities as we grow older is a sufficient indication of other limiting factors. But age also brings with it experience, wisdom and a deep appreciation of real freedom. This freedom is an inner freedom in the sense of feelings and meanings, rather than physically in the outer form. Can we not see that this is an echo of the limitless freedom of the infinite reality which is the cause of all creation?

Curious Distractions

We seek escape by turning to fortune telling, entertainment and other curious distractions.

The fact that we are not fully enthralled by the immense majesty and beauty of the ever-present reality is a proof that we are missing the point of the present, missing the meaning and experience of now, missing the point of being – which is beingness itself.

Curiosity implies a search, in order to fill a void or an emptiness which we feel. Entertainment is a common answer to the need to bring into one's life something that will cause pleasure, distraction or fulfilment. If we were already fulfilled and fully content with the present, if our cup were really full, we would not seek to fill it with distractions and trivialities.

Equally, looking towards the future with anxiety or expectation is a symptom of unfulfilment or discontent with the glorious present. So to turn towards fortune telling or astrology, to guess or hope for better times, means we are not able to see what is in front of us at this moment – perfect and just.

To see perfection in creational laws does not mean we have no role in improving the existential situation. The magnificent experience of the present includes both participation and awareness of the perfect underlying foundation – seeing two modes within a unified field.

Seeking the Supernatural

Man's natural disposition to seek a miracle or a glimpse into the unseen is a false substitute for the true ultimate miracle, which is the clear vision and the knowledge of the all-pervading reality, which is operative at all times and in all places.

Our interest in the supernatural arises from our failure to see the miraculous in the natural reality around us. In fact, to the eye of the enlightened seer, the supernatural is none other than the natural. It is only the limited horizon of the normal sensory perception that brings about the boundary between the physical world and the unseen.

However, the same way a keen eyesight can be developed by proper practice and care, insight too can be developed up to a point. Ultimately, we want to see in order to relate and understand. The supernatural is what normally lies beyond the knowledge and the perception of the ordinary self – not so for the superself!

Ali ibn Abi Talib reminds us that if we truly understand the natural world, we will discover the supra-natural behind it. If we catch a glimpse of the immense reality now, we will lose interest and concern about the future.

Love of the Old and the New

We see in our love of the old and the new, whether it be our love of old, precious objects or new possessions or fresh ideas, another aspect of the self's tendency towards its unific origin.

Regarding the old, we want to return to the starting-point, the beginning, for that is where our roots lie. Our love of antiques is only a milestone in our search for an entity which marks the beginning of time. There is something within us that constantly yearns for that which is the oldest in time, beyond time and not subject to time. The respect we have for old treasures and priceless antiques is a reflection of our search for the most ancient, the timeless. That is why we describe a priceless object as timeless!

Absolute reality transcends time, yet simultaneously contains it. Time emanates from it and is given a reality by virtue of its source of absolute reality. A fresh idea or a new object reminds us of this unific source because it is freshly born. It brings us closer to its source of origin. Every moment is the latest child of time, and time is a creature of timeless reality.

From non-existence comes existence. So any new existence reminds one more pointedly of where it has come from – its newness is a fresh reminder of absolute, all-encompassing timeless reality which brings about natural creations in time.

The Meaning of the Family Tree

In the same way, we all want to search for our roots and discover our ancestral lineage. The older we find our lineage to be, the more pleasing it is for us. The more prominent and renowned were our ancestors, the more pleasing that is too. The more virtuous, powerful, revered and loved were our ancestors, again the more pleased we are.

We look for the agreeable and admirable qualities of our ancestors when we search for our lineage. We wish to see high attributes in our origin. It is as though everyone wants to be a descendant of the best stock.

The truth is that all humanity descends from a spiritual origin whose attributes are noble and divinely related. So the real quest is to discover the source of all roots. Only then can we truly be inwardly proud and outwardly humble. Otherwise, the mere discovery of a noble ancestor may bring a false outer pride with the accompanying inner insecurity and uncertainty.

At the same time, we all wish to be content and pleased with our lineage no matter how humble or insignificant it is. We often find successful and self-assured people taking pride in their humble social or economic origins.

The paradox of our humble origin, and the satisfaction with and acceptance of it can be understood by deeper insight. It is not the ordinariness of the roots that makes one proud. It is the fact that we harbour a hidden treasure, an inner contentment and equilibrium irrespective of our hereditary origin. It is the finality that comes about when one is close to the root within the self, and not with the historical root. Searching for one's historical and hereditary root and getting over those facts will enable one more easily to attend to the real search at hand. The root here and now, the original throb in the heart once we turn sincerely towards its discovery! The unific source of all creation and roots!

Do Not Take the World for Granted

A valuable and wise counsel is not to take people and the world for granted or expect them to come up to one's expectations, otherwise one will be disappointed and suffer. This wisdom hides within it an insight into the fact that we do not belong to this physical, transient world. We cannot settle in this abode, we cannot rely on it. As we have seen earlier, there are constant uncertainties in this world, yet we seek certainty here and now.

The resolution of this contradiction can only come about if we recognise that permanency and reliability belong to another dimension or zone of experience. That dimension transcends time and space, for anything that exists in this world is subject to time and space, and is therefore inherently changeable – and thereby unreliable and uncertain.

We have seen that the world and its uncertainties are the fuel which propel the rocket of the self to search for the hidden dimension of certainty and inner security. The self, after disappointment with the world, may journey towards an appointment with discovery of itself. When the self discovers itself, self-knowledge is granted, and the natural world outside will never be taken for granted.

The Qur'an says, 'Surely they are at a loss who feel safe from Allah's plots'. It is self-deception if one thinks he has certainty where it concerns the affairs of this life, for no one is safe from change.

The Forty Days' Union

It is widely said that whoever keeps company with a group of people for forty days will become like one of them. Quite naturally, people extend bridges between themselves. Familiar points of contact and reference are established through familiarity and the recognition of similarities. One is certainly influenced by the company one keeps, taking on the colour of one's surroundings.

The natural tendency to connect with others in one's environment is a reflection of the truth that all human behaviour and knowledge is based on unity. Thus, when one wants to establish a human link, one looks for points which unite one to others. This process takes place both consciously and unconsciously. The unitive pulse inevitably works itself outward. We will relate to other persons and society if we stay long enough and near enough. The wise person, therefore, is one who keeps company with people of knowledge and light, and the fool is one who keeps company with fools. Birds of a feather do flock together.

According to the Qur'an, the Prophet Moses left the tribe of Israel for forty days of seclusion and meditation. It was during this time that he received further confirmation of his mission, returning as a true agent and representative of his Lord.

Sleep and Death

We all love deep sleep. We not only need sleep for health, we also desire and want it. Sleep restores our physical body, but more importantly, it enables the self to restore and re-energise itself – because the body's energy is derived from the soul which revives it.

Each night, the self steps aside from the body to regain its centrality and harmonise. It goes through a trial balance. We have seen earlier that sleep is like a trial run for death, a mini-death, yet, paradoxically, sleep is so desirable and death so frightening.

Deep sleep enables the body and all the systems within it to replenish and re-establish the appropriate equilibrium and stability to deal once again with the outside world. It restores the wholesome unity of the body.

Death is a more permanent form of sleep for the body. The self leaves it permanently, and the material elements which constituted the body are returned to earth, its original root. The self also returns to a state of consciousness not bound by time – from whence it originated. Now the union of each is complete and final, whereas the soul-body union in this life was only temporary and a prelude to this conclusion.

The Only Certainty

The only certainty in this life is that we will reach a certain point in this present existence – and this certain experience is death.

If death is the only certainty, then this fact somewhat begs the question, why do we not want to die? Why are we afraid of death? After all, from the moment of birth, every human being and living creature is already dying. There are no exceptions.

So whilst death is the most natural and universal occurrence, yet almost no human being looks forward to it. It is an unknown experience and we do not like unknowns. We quite naturally fear, dislike and avoid all unknowns. We hate death because we do not understand its nature. During this life we interact and interdepend on others. Death is non-dependence on anything.

However the reality of death is not total (inner) self-dependence, as was our primordial state before creation; but after death we enter another creation. After death we revert to total dependency upon the same absolute unific self from which we emanated and imagined our individual selfhood in this existence.

The final confirmed and stable certainty will come at the time of death, either in the voluntary sense (which is the death of the self and its desires) or in the natural sense, which is the biological death of the body.

Knowledge and experience of the certainty of death renders all other uncertainties of no importance.

Awakening and Spiritual Maturity

With maturity and advancing age, the horizon is expanded, wisdom increased and the possibility of inner awakening nearer. The examples below point to the return of the higher self to its unific origin.

Ending at the Beginning

We find that the older we grow and the nearer we are to death, the more we remember our youth and our earliest years. We all go through to varying intensities the process of retracing the events of our life in flashback, to our root or origin. Because the end and the beginning are not separate, we want to connect the present with the past.

Our early impressions, emotions and mental images leave a crucial mark upon us which begins to be highlighted with age. It seems that the older an experience is the greater is the impact upon us. Extending this observation back to the point of human inception and prior to that, we can rationally conclude that the unknown, unseen factors or laws governing natural creation, with particular reference to the individual, must be of major significance in human life.

This is why, as we approach death, we look back on our life's experiences in order to try to get near to the source of creation. But the same source is present now, and in the future. It is this search for the primal, unific origin that propels us to look at the past, present and future. The Qur'an says that man's physicality was created from earth and to the earth it shall return, and his spirit by the Creator's decree and to the Creator it shall return.

Love of Nature

Another indication of our unific being can be seen in our love and admiration of nature – of the wilderness, forests, mountains, the countryside, vast oceans and the desert. We are attracted to these natural scenes and environments because they have their own organic and unifying systems and are reflections and physical manifestations of a natural ecological unity that is primal, organic and self-sustaining. The harmony, balance and stability of these natural creations are a reminder of the unitive programme within our heart.

We observe that natural phenomena have their own way of maintaining and caring for themselves, whilst reflecting the beautiful, glorious and all-pervading reality behind them. Nature is ever so true in its adoration and submission to that reality.

So our love and communion with nature are a reminder of the vast ecosystem which rules over all systems. It is a reflection that reminds us of that which is already within us – that primordial ocean of perfect unity, self-regulated and everlasting.

Our love and contemplation of nature are an aspect of our love for and reflection upon what is within the self. The blueprint of natural creation is engraved within our inner being, ever present. The Qur'an and the Prophetic traditions recommend the contemplation and study of nature in all its multitudinous harmony, in order to see the divine attributes of beauty and perfection, both on the horizon and within oneself.

The Journey in Life

In conclusion, then, the journey in life is the manifest confirmation of the eternal blueprint. When the wayfarer discovers the reality of the self, acknowledges the creational blueprint at hand and confirms experientially the natural bounds, the rest of the journey is only a reconfirmation of that truth, both inner and outer. The map at hand will be seen to encompass the rest of creation in this existence.

The first part of the journey is to gain certainty, and confirmation of the truth which will emanate from self-knowledge. Then comes the growth in self-realisation, both in extent and depth. This pattern of growth and evolvement reflects the total unitive power which is behind all systems and creations.

So the journey is none other than reading the map in one's hand and seeing its parallel in outer existence everywhere one goes – no matter to which culture, place, or people – to see the same patterns repeating with a slightly different shade of colour and texture; otherwise the basic underlying structure is the same, because the original root and source is one.

A journey is only meaningful when there is an objective, and a map or plan to follow. The objective we already have in our innate being. There are those scintillating moments when one is completely in unison with totality. The rest of the time on the journey is taken up with reading the map and transposing it upon the geography outside.

We have been given a blueprint of self-knowledge that applies to all humanity, for use by humanity, which contains the story of humanity. It outlines our journey in this life which is based on duality. It confirms our spiritual origin from one essence and describes our true nature and potential. If we awaken to this knowledge, then we have saved ourselves and are transformed. If we do not awaken to it, we are misguided, groping in the dark and grasping at any straw: a life wasted, and a disastrous journey.

The treatment and cure of the self is only a stepping-stone, a take-off point, towards a higher realm for which we have been brought into this world to be trained to attain. In itself, the cure is not the end. The training and discipline for our journey involves uplifting the self to a translucent, purified and transformed condition by means of cleansing the heart. In this state the subtle, intuitive, primal intelligence in us is awakened, and complements the mental processes of logic and causality. As self-awareness and reflection begin to develop, an expansion of consciousness and intuitive behaviour are experienced. This state is only a beginning and not an end. Our training can only bring us to the boundary of the world of pure consciousness and absolute beingness, and that is the world to which we will return after death. It is this experientially attainable state to which we all aspire – that point is the journey's end and true life's beginning.

So the cure of the self is undertaken in order for it to explore and experience another realm, and that is why, no matter how far a person progresses in this world in his outer or inner achievements, he will still not be satisfied, for basically we are in this world but not of it. Our form may be limited, and may follow the most logical laws and regulations, but our essence is freer than anything we can imagine; it is free of all limitations.

The way actually to experience the essence cannot be totally described. We can use paths, practices and prescriptions in order to reach the boundary of higher consciousness, to be at a stage from which we can only step into that absolute realm – not by effort or will anymore, but by the mercy of the ultimate, the source of all creation. So at least we can journey to the gate of the Garden of Paradise! When, how and by whom the door opens is not our business. That event may happen when absolute unitive power prevails and the microself is overwhelmed by the one self.

We have seen that life in the abstract as well as the subjective sense is given great value, because its source is from a realm that is absolute, timeless, unified and sacred. We also know that in the subjective sense, life as we experience it is short-lived. We all share within ourselves a certain urge to discover the purpose of life, the significance of this existence and what lies behind it. So life is given the supreme value and the greatest meaning, because its purpose is to discover its essence and its origin, the all-embracing, all-loving life-giver.

One of the essential steps towards the discovery of the meaning of life is the actual discovery and experience of death within ourselves. This is the death of meaning, the death of utter and absolute silence, before biological death. Once it is experienced, once we have touched upon the state of pure consciousness and bliss, from that point on we shall be able to face physical death in a more rational and stable way, and shall not be frightened of the experience of death as such. Knowledge removes all fears. From then on, the urgency of discovery and deep respect for life drives one along the ocean of mercy and compassion towards greater self-fulfilment.

Most questions relating to human life can be easily answered according to our model of the self, and thus we gain self-knowledge. The meaning and value of life is a key question. Life has been given the highest value, and is the greatest treasure given to humankind, because it emanates from the unific sacred source. No one has the right to extinguish it as long as it throbs in one's heart. There is no question that the gift of life and the diverse experience of living are given as a sacred right in order to discover the sacred origin.

A Prophetic tradition states this: 'I [God] was a hidden treasure and I loved to be known, therefore I created, so I could be known.' Another Prophetic tradition relates that he who knows himself, truly he knows his Lord.

So the unique, unific treasure in its absolute beingness created out of love, so that it could be adored. The vehicle for that discovery is the self itself, and the fuel is self-knowledge. If we put this in front of our eyes, then every aspect of this existence becomes purposeful, meaningful and manageable. For once we have observed the divine transcendent beauty and majesty in creation, we wish to remain in that state. The truth is that we are already in that unified state, but it is up to us to remain conscious of it. This is the choice given to us.

Hopefully, this book has shown us the eternal spring of limitless freedom within us, the source of that spring and the stepping-stones by which we can reach that source.

There is nothing new in our search for freedom. There is nothing new in our ability to reach that state of limitless freedom, and there is nothing new in the fact that the only way to that freedom is by our submission to truth and thereby awakening to it. The only new dimension is time itself, for the moment never repeats. It is forever fresh and new.

As Ali ibn Abi Talib said, 'You are the evident book by whose signs that which was hidden becomes apparent'. The greatest puzzle is that the eternal secret is ever effulgent. But are our eyes strong enough to look at the sun?

So we exemplify that infinite reality from which we were created. We can say that we have no end, and we have no beginning. Yet in this life there is a physical beginning and an end. The opposite must also exist. Our real beginning was from an infinite zone. Our present is encapsulated in time, and our end will again be within the infinite.

From the finite experience of life we can glimpse the infinite behind it. Our sight needs to be strengthened to look at the sun. Once the winter of ignorance and darkness is passed, the spring light of consciousness brings its colourful delights – pure delight by yourself, for yourself, from yourself. All of this unending love and mercy emanating from the One creator who commanded the self to be, Allah ta'ala.

Notes

Chapter Two: The Nature and Spectrum of the Self

1. Sayyid Sharif al-Jurjani, the fourteenth-century Persian theologian and gnostic.
2. Sadr al-Din Muhammad al-Shirazi, widely known as Mulla Sadra, the sixteenth-century Persian gnostic and theosopher.
3. Known as Avicenna in the West, Ibn Sina lived in the eleventh century in Bokhara (in present day Russia).
4. Nasir al-Din abu Jafar al-Tusi, the thirteenth-century Persian ethical philosopher.
5. Ahmad ibn Muhammad al-Miskawayh, a historian and philosopher of the tenth century in Iran.
6. View held by Sayyid M. H. Tabataba'i, the twentieth-century theologian and scholar of Iran.
7. The fourth Islamic caliph and first Shi'ite Imam, the renowned seventh-century master, gnostic and traditionist to whom all Sufi orders trace their origin.

Chapter Three: The Journey of the Self

1. See *Journey of the Universe as expounded in the Qur'an*, by the author, published by KPI Ltd, London: 1985, for a detailed account of the story of creation.
2. The grid of opposites has been based on the teachings of the eighteenth-century Moroccan gnostic, Sidi Ali al-Jamal, as described in *The Meaning of Man* by Sidi Ali al-Jamal, published by Diwan Press, Norwich (UK): 1977.

3. Ahmad ibn Muhammad al-Miskawayh, the tenth-century ethical philosopher of Iran.
4. The fourth Islamic caliph, and first Shi'ite Imam, the renowned seventh-century master, gnostic and traditionist to whom all Sufi orders trace their origin.
5. Rabi'ah al-Adawiya bint Ismail, the eighth-century saint of Basra, Iraq.
6. Sadr al-Din Muhammad al-Shirazi, widely known as Mulla Sadra, the renowned sixteenth-century Persian theosopher.
7. The intention, meaning and source of all creation.
8. This is the same event that is referred to in Christianity as the Day of Judgement.
9. Muhyiddin ibn Arabi, or al-Arabi, sixteenth-century theologian and mystic of Andalusia, Spain.

Chapter Four: Treatment, Cure and Fulfilment

1. Ahmad ibn Muhammad al-Miskawayh, tenth-century Persian ethical philosopher.
2. Nasir al-Din al-Tusi, thirteenth-century Persian philosopher.
3. Abu Yusuf Yaqub ibn Ishaq al-Kindi, ninth-century philosopher of Baghdad.
4. Abu Bakr Muhammad ibn Zakariyya al-Razi, known in the West as Rhazes, tenth-century Persian theologian and physician.
5. Expounded by Dhu al-Nun al-Misri, ninth-century Egyptian gnostic.

Authors Quoted

1. Al-Adawiya, Rabi'ah bint Ismail; the eighth-century saint of Basra, Iraq.
2. Al-Jamal, Sidi Ali; eighteenth-century Moroccan gnostic who described the grid of opposites in *The Meaning of Man*, published by Diwan Press, Norwich (UK): 1977.
3. Al-Jurjani, Sayyid Sharif; the fourteenth-century Persian theologian and gnostic.
4. Al-Kindi, Abu Yusuf Yaqub ibn Ishaq; ninth-century philosopher of Baghdad.
5. Al-Miskawayh, Ahmad ibn Muhammad; a historian and philosopher of the tenth century in Iran.
6. Al-Misri, Dhu al-Nun; ninth-century Egyptian gnostic.
7. Al-Razi, Abu Bakr Muhammad ibn Zakariyya; known in the West as Rhazes, tenth-century Persian theologian and physician.
8. Al-Shirazi, Sadr al-Din Muhammad; widely known as Mulla Sadra, the renowned sixteenth-century Persian theosopher.
9. Al-Tusi, Nasir al-Din abu Jafar; the thirteenth-century Persian ethical philosopher.
10. Ibn Abi Talib, Ali; the fourth Islamic caliph and first Shi'ite Imam, the renowned seventh-century master, gnostic and traditionist to whom all Sufi orders trace their origin.
11. Ibn Arabi, Muhyiddin; or al-Arabi, sixteenth-century theologian and mystic of Andalusia, Spain.
12. Ibn Sina; known as Avicenna in the West, lived in the eleventh century in Bokhara (in present day Russia).

Bibliography

Ādab al-nafs, by al-'Ālim al-Sayyid Muḥammad al-Aytānī; edited by Sayyid Kāzim al-Mūsawī, Tehran: al-Maktabah al-Raḍawīyah, 1280 H./1863.

al-Asfār al-'arba'ah (al-Ḥikmah al-muta'ālīyah fī al-asfār al-'aqlīyah al-'arba'ah), by Ṣadr al-Dīn Muḥammad ibn Ibrāhīm al-Shīrāzī, Beirut: Dār Iḥyā' al-Turāth al-'Arabī, n.d.

Asrār al-āyāt, by Ṣadr al-Dīn Muḥammad ibn Ibrāhīm al-Shīrāzī; edited by Muḥammad Khwājavī, Tehran: Anjuman-i Islāmī-i Ḥikmat, 1360s./1981.

Asrār al-sharī'ah wa-aṭwār al-ṭarīqah wa-anwār al-ḥaqīqah, by al-Sayyid Ḥaydar al-Amulī; edited by Muḥammad Khwājavī, Tehran: Mu'assasah-i Muṭāla'āt va Taḥqīqāt-i Farhangī, 1403 H./1983.

Dirāsah fī al-mashākil al-akhlāqīyah wa-al-nafsīyah, by Mujtabā al-Mūsa-wī al-Lārī; translated into Arabic by Muḥammad Hādī al-Gharawī, Tehran: Maktab-i Nashr al-Intiqām al-Islām, 1405 H./1984.

al-Futūḥat al-Makkīyah, by al-Shaykh al-Akbar Muḥyī al-Dīn ibn ᶜArabī al-Ḥātimī, Beirut: Dār Iḥyā' al-Turāth al-'Arabī, n.d.

al-Ḥaqā'iq fī maḥāsin al-akhlāq [with] Qurrat al-'uyūn fī al-ma'ārif wa-al-ḥikam, by al-Fayḍ al-Kāshānī, Beirut: Dār al-Kitāb al-'Arabī, n.d.

al-Ḥikmah al-muta'ālīyah fī al-asfār al-'aqlīyah al-'arba'ah, by Ṣadr al-Dīn Muḥammad ibn Ibrāhīm al-Shīrāzī, Beirut: Dār Iḥyā' al-Turāth al-'Arabī, n.d.

'Ilal al-sharā'i, by al-Shaykh al-Ṣadūq, Beirut: Dār Iḥyā' Turāth al-'Arabī, 1966.

al-Insān al-kāmil fī ma'rifat al-awākhir wa-al-awā'il, by al-Shaykh 'Abd al-Karīm al-Jīlī, Cairo: Maktabat Muṣṭafā al-Bābī, n.d.

Īqāẓ al-nā'imīn, by Ṣadr al-Dīn Muḥammad ibn Ibrāhīm al-Shīrāzī; edited by Muḥsin Mu'ayyadī, Tehran: Mu'assasah-i Muṭāla'āt va Taḥqīqāt-i Farhangī, n.d.

al-Ishārāt wa-al-tanbīhāt, by al-Shaykh Abū 'Alī Ḥusayn ibn 'Abd Allāh Ibn Sīnā, with commentary of Naṣir al-Dīn al-Ṭūsī and a super commentary of 'Allāmah Quṭb al-Dīn Muḥammad al-Rāzī, 2nd ed., Iran: Daftar-i Nashr-i Kitāb, 1403 H./1982.

Jāmi' al-sa'ādāt, by al-Shaykh Muḥammad Mahdī al-Narāqī, Baghdād: Dār al-Nu'mān, n.d.

Kitāb al-mashā'ir, by Ṣadr al-Dīn Muḥammad ibn Ibrāhīm al-Shīrāzī, Isfahan: Intishārāt-i Mahdavī, n.d.

Kitāb al-shifā, by Ḥusayn ibn 'Abd Allāh Ibn Sīnā; edited by Maḥmūd Qāsim and Ibrāhīm Madkūr, Cairo: Dār al-Kātib al-'Arabī, 1389–95 H./1969–1975.

Kitāb al-ta'rifāt, by al-Sayyid al-Sharīf 'Alī ibn Muḥammad al-Jurjānī, Tehran: Dār al-Kutub al-'Ilmīyah, n.d.

Makārim al-akhlāq, by al-Shaykh Raḍī al-Dīn al-Ṭabarsī, Beirut: Mu'assasah al-'Alamī, 1972.

al-Mīzān fī tafsīr al-Qur'ān, by al-'Allāmah Muḥammad Ḥusayn al-Ṭabāṭabā'ī, Beirut: Mu'assasah al-'Alamī, 1973.

al-Mukhallaṣ fī tazkīyah al-nafs, by Sa'īd Ḥawī, Cairo and Beirut: Dār al-Islām, 1975.

Nafḥat al-rūḥ wa-tuḥfat al-futūḥ, by Mu'ayyad al-Dīn Janadī, Tehran: Intishārāt-i Mawlā, 1403 H./1982.

Nasirean Ethics, by Nasir al Din al-Tusi; translated from original Persian by G. M. Wickens, London: G. Allen and Unwin, 1964.

Nūr al-ḥaqīqah wa-nūr al-ḥadīqah fī 'ilm al-akhlāq, by 'Izz al-Dīn al-Ḥusayn ibn 'Abd al-Ṣamad al-Ḥārithī al-Hamdānī al-'Āmilī [Father of Al-Shaykh al-Bahā'ī]; edited by Muḥammad Jawād al-Ḥusaynī al-Jalālī, Qum: Maṭba'at-i Mihr, n.d.

Rāḥat al-'aql, by Aḥmad Ḥamīd al-Dīn al-Kirmānī; edited by Muṣṭafā Ghālib, Beirut: Dār al-Andalus, 1967.

The Refinement of Character, by Ahmad ibn Muhammad Miskawayh; translated from original Arabic by Constantine K. Zurayk, Beirut: American University of Beirut, 1968.

Sadr al-Din Shirazi and His Transcendent Theosophy, by Seyyed Hossein Nasr, Tehran: Imperial Iranian Academy of Philosophy, 1978.

al-Shawāhid al-rubūbīyah fī manāhij al-sulūkīyah, by Ṣadr al-Dīn al-Shīrāzī Muḥammad ibn Ibrāhīm; edited by Jalāl al-Dīn Āshtiyānī, Tehran: s.n., n.d.

The Spiritual Physick of Rhazes, by Abū Bakr Muḥammad ibn al-Zakarīyā^c al-Rāzī; translated from original Arabic by Arthur J. Arberry, London: John Murray, 1950.

The Tao of Physics, by Fritjof Capra, London: Flamingo Edition of Fontana Paperbacks, 14th reprint, 1988.

Index

Shaykh Fadhlalla Haeri was born in Kerbala, Iraq, a descendant of several generations of well-known, revered spiritual leaders. Educated in the West, he embarked upon a successful business career, primarily as a consultant in the oil industry. His extensive travelling led to his rediscovery of the Islamic heritage of his birth. Shaykh Fadhlalla has established a number of charitable and publishing organisations and is the author of several books.